WORKING @ HOME

WORKING AND LIVING SPACES

WORKING AND LIVING SPACES

W@H

Publisher	Paco Asensio
Editor and text	Aurora Cuito
Translation	Harry Paul
Copy-editing	Wendy Griswold
Proofreading	Bill Bain
Art Director	Mireia Casanovas Soley
ISBN Softcover	0-8230-5870-0
ISBN Hardcover	0-06-018482-5
Printed in Spain	Gràfiques Ibèria S.A.

2000 © Loft Publications S.L. and HBI, an imprint of HarperCollins Publishers

First published in 2000 by LOFT and HBI, an imprint of HarperCollins Publishers 10 East 53rd St. New York, NY 10022-5299

Distributed in the U.S. and Canada by Watson-Guptill Publications 770 Broadway New York, NY 10003-9595
Ph.: (800) 451-1741 or (732) 363-4511 in NJ, AK, HI
Fax: (732) 363-0338

Distributed throughout the rest of the world by HarperCollins International 10 East 53rd St. New York, NY 10022-5299
Fax: (212) 207-7654

Illustration back cover	© Berto Martínez
Title page	© Toni Quesada

If you would like to suggest projects for inclusion in our next volumes, please e-mail details to us at: loft@loftpublications.com

Introduction

Like the Bohemian artists of times gone by, an increasing number of people are establishing their workplaces at home. At the beginning of the century, painters and sculptors practiced their art in the same location where they ate, rested, and slept, and so were able to return to their work whenever a flash of inspiration came to them. Naturally, they also avoided having to pay two rents.

Nowadays there are many reasons why professionals decide to install offices in their residences. First and foremost, travel is eliminated. Urban sprawl means that a lot of commuters are wasting hours and hours in their cars or jammed into trains getting to work. In addition, strict schedules are incompatible with domestic chores and make night workers weary in the morning, too jaded to be at their best. Finally, often eight hours or more of professional dedication are required. If the environment is not comfortable, warm, and inviting, the work can become nightmarish drudgery. Tests have shown that work performance and job satisfaction in an office vary greatly according to the layout, decor, and furniture.

Without a doubt, working from home provides much more freedom and allows one to enjoy an individualized schedule which can be reconciled with other activities. The worker has no need to commute and can create a made-to-measure environment, in accordance with his or her needs and desires.

The conditions which have brought about these social changes should be noted. The information technology revolution has improved the speed and efficiency of communication: vast amounts of information can be sent in a split second. Furthermore, intense specialization and the emergence of new professions mean that many people are not limited when it comes to choosing where to work.

This book concentrates on the design of multi-purpose homes which simultaneously meet domestic and professional requirements. The projects, designed by prestigious international architects, have been selected because they offer ingenious solutions which accommodate two completely distinct and seemingly incompatible purposes at the same site.

Some designers have decided to avoid direct contact between the domestic and professional purposes and have therefore placed the studio in one structure and the residence in another, a few yards apart. Others have preferred to utilize different floors, linking rooms with staircases or ramps. Finally, there are creators who, because of the express desire of their clients or space limitations, have mixed functions in a versatile space divided by indistinct boundary lines.

The intent behind all the projects in this book is the creation of a welcoming and flexible ambience: domestic spaces where work, in addition to being a necessity, is a pleasure.

Prologue

The dream ship

In this book, we are going to explain several times how the information technology revolution has provided the opportunity to work at home. This project by Koeppel and Martínez takes advantage of this opportunity, applying revolutionary architectural ideas to it. Spite its experimental nature, which is light years away from conventional homes, it has been included in this prologue because it shows a willingness to take bold risks and is a vote of confidence in favor of tomorrow's architecture. Its extravagance does not neglect the functionality needed by the clients.

In Navia, next to the mouth of the river which gives the town its name, an old, restored windmill reveals nothing about the activities of its three inhabitants, artists who communicate with the world via the Internet from this remote outpost in the northern Spanish province of Asturias. In a rustic landscape of green pastures and rocky ground, next to a railroad track, this structure-now a studio and home- will soon have an unusual, even bizarre neighbor: a pavilion/apartment with the profile of a spaceship which invites you to depart for the virtual world of dreams.

Inspired by a traditional granary which the clients had planned to equip and furnish, the pavilion

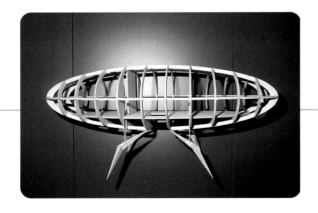

contains two bedrooms, an entrance hall, and a bathroom in a pod-like, elliptical capsule on semi-flexed metal legs. Inside is an open space providing a comfortable, relaxing ambiance. The only way to reach the ground is by a stairway which can be folded away to provide isolation from the world. Christened the NAVE (Net Access Virtual Embarking), this architectural pioneer was designed for many possible uses: projection theater, workshop, bar, or library. Its structure brings to mind an aircraft hangar. Stretched canvas covers laminated wood. The prototype, displayed next to Lake Constance when the Bregenz Kunsthaus was inaugurated, eschewed windows,

replacing them with monitors connected to the virtual world. In the Austrian museum, the pavilion was finished with a silver-colored, lacquered canvas because the experimental waterproof but transpirable material which was to have been used failed to pass its tests before the opening.

The interior, in plaster applied directly onto the mesh, is insulated by shredded paper among the wiring. In central Europe, the structure was taken down and transferred to Asturias, Spain. There, the rooms will enjoy the sun through the skylights. Soon, the patient clients will receive their reward when their dreams ship arrives.

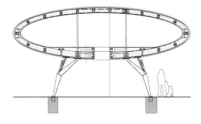  

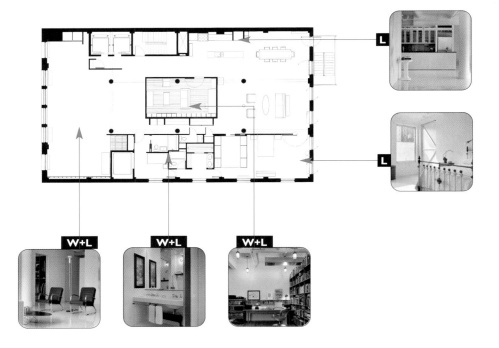

THE SIEGEL-SWANSEA LOFT

Architects: Abelow Connors
Sherman Architects
Collaborator: Marcus Donagh
Location: New York City, U.S.A.
Date of construction: 1997
Photographs: Michael Moran
Area: 2,150 sq. feet

WRITING AND PAINTING IN A LOFT Abelow Connors Sherman Architects

Writer Joel Siegel and his wife, painter Ena Swansea, bought this New York City loft to create a space where they could both live and work. They wanted to integrate seemingly incompatible aesthetic and functional influences to produce a flexible domestic and work environment. The original character of the building, an early twentieth-century factory, was respected. The vaulted ceiling, plastered walls, and industrial details were retained. Restoration work employed similar products and materials, and electrical installations and pipes were left exposed. These subtly emphasized the original features of the building, while the latest techniques were used to rigorously and precisely accent each detail.

The north-facing studio allows the artist to contemplate panoramic views through the large windows, inspiring when the sun edges out from behind the clouds or beats down on clear days. Its space opens into the living area. But there is no direct visual link because the office occupies the center of the loft, a space for relaxation and entertainment as well as for writing and painting. The essentials are there (bookcase, table, chair) as well as a state-of-the-art sound and television system, a computer, and multimedia gadgets.

This is a private domain; the couple unwinds here. So it is visually and acoustically isolated from the rest of the dwelling. The separation is underscored by the fact that it is the only room in which the wood flooring was preserved, which makes it an island surrounded by the rest of the apartment.

The most private areas, the bedrooms, bathrooms, and dressing room, are on the edges, partitioned off from the other areas. The kitchen, dining room, and living room mingle with the studio, entrance hall, and corridor.

The original floor was covered with an epoxy-urethane compound. To avoid excessive color, the vertical partitions were finished with a filler which produced a grayish, balanced, neutral ambience so the artwork can be fully appreciated in color and form.

The living room. The art pieces have been painted by the owner.

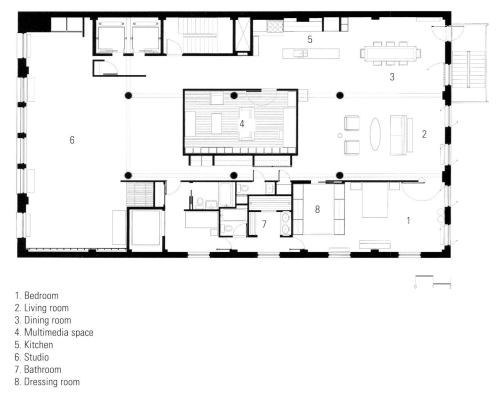

1. Bedroom
2. Living room
3. Dining room
4. Multimedia space
5. Kitchen
6. Studio
7. Bathroom
8. Dressing room

The kitchen, dining room, and living room blend into the studio which is located right next to the large windows. The magnificent views of the city are always a source of inspiration for the artist.

Writing space.

Paintings by Ena Swansea.

Top: view of the open kitchen. Bottom: the bedroom is decorated in white as is most of the apartment. Right: Detail of the bathroom sink.

The neutral finishes allow the furniture and art objects to come to the fore. Plants and small decorative embellishments add a touch of color to the predominant white of the dwelling, the rustic details contrasting with the general industrial appearance.

First floor

Second floor

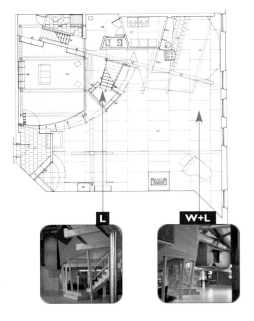

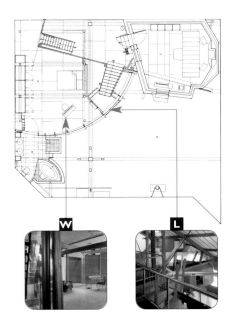

JERSEY CITY LOFT

Architects: Abelow Connors
Sherman Architects
Collaborator: David Younglove
Location: Jersey City,
New Jersey, U.S.A.
Date of construction: 1993
Photographs: Michael Moran
Area: 2,400 sq. feet

A MUSICIAN'S STUDIO AND HOME   Abelow Connors Sherman Architects

This Jersey City project is noteworthy for the industrial nature of the design and the diversity of materials and construction elements employed. The building was a warehouse and stable dating from 1880, with a sloping ceiling, web of beams, wooden pillars, and brick walls. These features were retained, and period pieces were added as recollections of the past. The architects wanted to remain true to the spirit of the building, so they concentrated their efforts on the functional requirements of the home and workplace.

The client, a musician and producer, needed all the conventional domestic features plus an office and a fully-equipped recording studio. The designers set themselves the task of creatively synthesizing everyday functions with the client's professional activities.

The acoustics of both the living space and the recording studio are enhanced by the three-story-high ceiling. The kitchen, dining room, library, and computer room are also on the first floor, while the two upper floors contain bedrooms and the control/sound-mixing room. Private and work spaces are side by side throughout the house.

The shape of the dwelling permits vertical and horizontal connections between the overall structure and the new forms. Movable panels and openings in some of the walls allow certain rooms to be combined. The client's lifestyle demands flexibility in which home adapts to the changing scene.

The materials used vary with the components. Galvanized metal accents one of the walls. For the pillars, structural beams, and some of the finishes, wood seemed the best bet. The curved wall called for suppler wood. The variety of materials enhances the extraordinary nature of the entire project.

Axonometric perspective

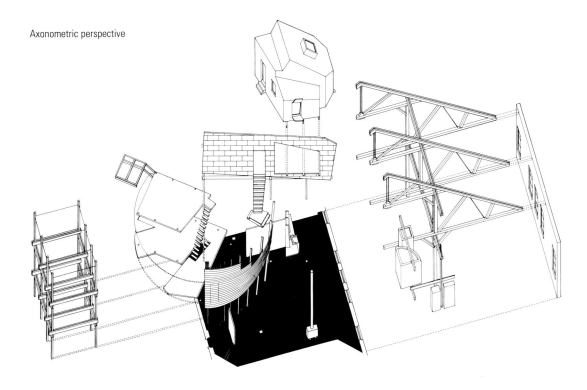

Left: view of the project from the entrance. Right: the multi-use character of the space is especially evident on this floor, where elements involving distinct activities can be seen: a piano, basketball hoop, library, and kitchen.

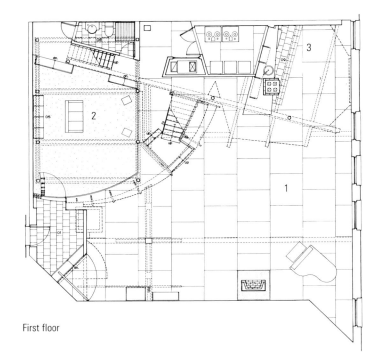

First floor

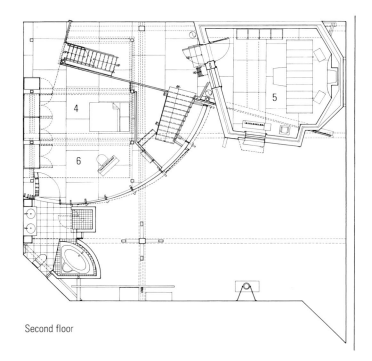

Second floor

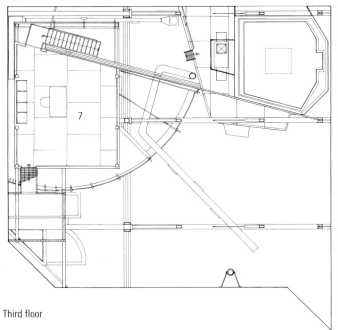
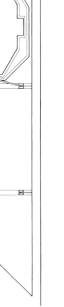

Third floor

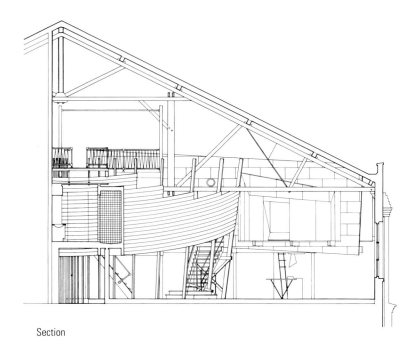

Section

1. Multiuse room
2. Living room
3. Kitchen
4. Bedroom

5. Production studio
6. Rehearsing room
7. Multiuse studio

0   1   2

The images on this page show the stairs, made with iron cables and wooden steps. The balcony on this floor overlooks the whole project.

Left: this section shows the room layout in the large, irregular space. Distribution elements added to the industrial structure form a heterogeneous unit.

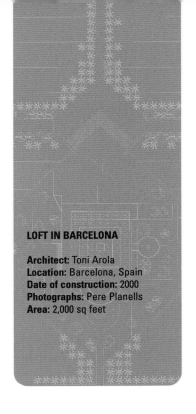

LOFT IN BARCELONA

Architect: Toni Arola
Location: Barcelona, Spain
Date of construction: 2000
Photographs: Pere Planells
Area: 2,000 sq feet

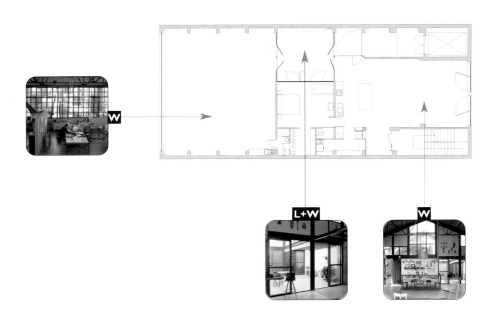

RENOVATED INDUSTRIAL SPACE FOR A DESIGNER   Toni Arola

Like New York's Soho, the industrial area of Poblenou in Barcelona has gradually become the favorite place of architects and artists. The spaciousness, high ceilings, and abundant light have seduced many professionals into relocating to the old factories and warehouses. The expansive interiors encouraged most to live and work in the same place, including the renowned graphic and industrial designer Toni Arola, who decided to restore an old factory and turn it into a residence and workshop.

The space is divided into two large rooms, one for his work team and the other for his private life, separated by a small patio. Motivated by his desire for flexibility, Arola designed a space which can evolve in accordance with whatever demands might arise. He also envisions building an attic as well as a terrace between the roofs.

Enormous windows on the façade and the glass facing the patio ensure that, in both studio and home, sunlight for daily activities is never lacking. The lighting is enhanced by lamps designed by Arola.

The original wood structure, ironwork, and unpainted metal frames were preserved, evoking the factory ambience and giving the space a constantly changing allure.

In both the workshop and private areas, the designer's personality is communicated through his special collection, including his own designs, of African and Oriental artwork, precious stones, and branches found in the countryside. Arola gives special attention to things shaped by the persistent action of nature, for he himself works by sculpting objects, not by brute force, but with delicate care, constantly refining an idea until a beautiful, practical form is created.

Partial view of the working area.

Right: the home is an open-plan space where different functions coexist: the living room, dining room, and worktable...
Top: panels and sliding doors, which provide needed privacy, separate the rooms.

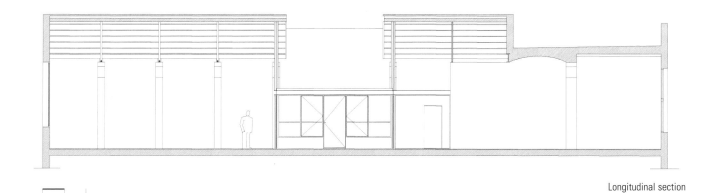

Longitudinal section

Layout

1. Studio
2. Patio
3. Bedroom
4. Dressing room
5. Bathroom
6. Kitchen
7. Living room

Left: entrance hall,
patio and views of the
living and working areas.

View of the patio from the interior.

Previous page: as in the rest of the home, objects, stones, drawings, and sculptures are exhibited in the bathroom.

Top: a collection of perfume bottles designed by Toni Arola provides the final detail for this curious bathroom showcase.

Left: view of the bedroom and the dining room, where the original ceiling of the house can be seen.

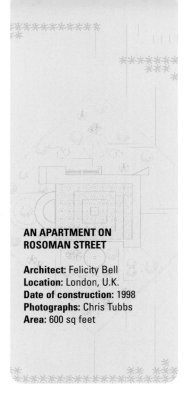

**AN APARTMENT ON
ROSOMAN STREET**

Architect: Felicity Bell
Location: London, U.K.
Date of construction: 1998
Photographs: Chris Tubbs
Area: 600 sq feet

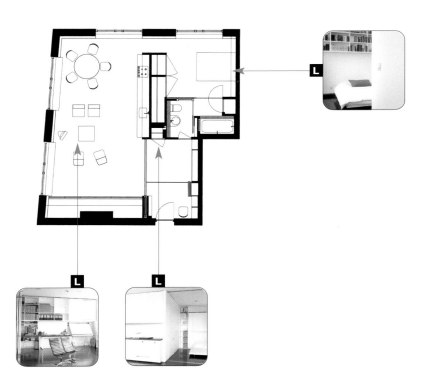

A VERSATILE RESIDENCE FOR TWO DESIGNERS   Felicity Bell

This apartment in the Borough of Clerkenwell, London, was created as a home and studio for interior designers Felicity Bell and Christian Papa. From the beginning, great effort was made to preserve the feeling of light and space, and to provide a work area and meeting room without destroying the sense of intimacy. The solution was a series of sliding screens which, when closed, provide small private spaces for guests and clients, but which open to reveal a large, unobstructed area.

The building's industrial nature had little influence on the project's outcome, since the space was essentially neutral. This was particularly attractive because of the need for functionality. The woodwork, finishes, and framing were modified to tone down the factory appearance and introduce a more contemporary look.

The floor is divided by an imaginary center line. On one side is a wide, flexible area for living and working, and on the other is the master bedroom with bath. Two translucent screens near the entrance are normally folded back, allowing unobstructed movement. Slide one screen across, however, and the passage becomes a meeting room. Accordingly, business can be conducted without the visitors seeing the private home.

A hidden door in the entrance hall leads to the bathroom, which can also be divided, with one area being kept private if desired. Still another screen, in combination with a bed and mattress which fold efficiently out of the wall, creates a guest bedroom. The entrance hall cupboard serves as a wardrobe, and the bath is shared with the master bedroom.

Along one of the walls in the main area, work space has been set up, with a work table, shelves, and drawing table. This area can be hidden by more folding screens.

The light-filled kitchen tucks gleaming appliances away in cupboards. Work surfaces are made of jarrah, a highly decorative, intensely colored wood from Australia. The gray rubber floor offsets the natural luster of the apartment.

The plans show the different layouts the apartment can have. The entrance hall can also be used as a meeting room or guest bedroom.

1. Main bedroom
2. Dinning area
3. Kitchen
4. Living room
5. Office
6. Entrance
7. Meeting room
8. Guest bedroom

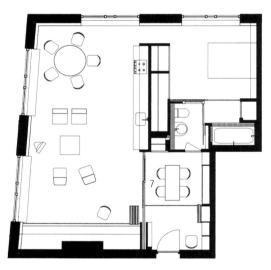

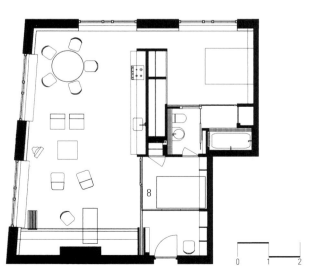

0   1   2

Bottom: view of the living room. Right: the studio when the folding screens are open. The shelves and the work table can be seen.

Shown on the left are the sliding doors that conceal the office, library, files, and two tables, including one for drawing. When housework is being done or other tasks in the residents' private lives are being performed, the studio is closed off to avoid interruption.

This room can be used as a reception area, meeting room or a bedroom for guests.

On the right, the next room contains a fold-away bed. This is one of many devices that enhance this flexible, multiuse home.

THE CAMPANA LOFT

Architect: Fernando Campana
Location: São Paulo, Brazil
Date of construction: 1997
Photographs: Andrés Ortero
Area: 2,475 sq. feet

A MULTIPURPOSE SPACE IN SÃO PAULO Fernando Campana

L iving in a loft is a new concept in Brazil. However, with restaurants, shops, and clubs changing the face of former factory areas, decades-old commercial buildings are being renovated for domestic use. This project by Fernando Campana, in a 1940s commercial building in the middle of a residential district in downtown São Paulo, serves as a studio, exhibition space, and residence. When the architect, also a renowned furniture designer, started work, the concrete block building was in two parts at the front and rear of the plot, joined by common bathrooms. Campana converted the second floor of the front section into a large exhibition area and living space.

The rear of the building became a workshop and kitchen. The lower floor was transformed into a bedroom with bath. The old toilets were demolished to make way for a magnificent open-air patio.

To ensure optimal lighting in the exhibition area, a large steel-framed window was installed in the back wall, affording a view of the subtly-landscaped patio. Unpretentious finishes were used inside to preserve the rough industrial ambience. The walls were covered with thick plaster and painted, while the concrete floors were waxed and polished, and the concrete staircase was left untouched to enhance the overall factory feel.

By designing the furniture himself, Campana sought to link the entire project stylistically and, indeed, the pieces stand out as works of art in their own right. Initially, the building was envisioned only as a space for exhibitions and a workshop for prototypes, but after finishing it the architect realized that it was flexible enough to double as a dwelling. There was plenty of neutral space to accommodate different functions throughout the day.

The atelier.

Shown are different views of the project: the façade of the building and interior areas, including the patio and the living room. Most of the furniture was designed by Fernando Campana himself.

To the right: the back wall is a large steel frame façade that ensures sunlight to the exhibition hall.

**LIPSCHUTZ-JONES
APARTMENT**

Architects: Frank Lupo
and Daniel Rowen
Location: New York City, U.S.A.
Date of construction: 1998
Photographs: Michael Moran
Area: 1,600 sq. feet

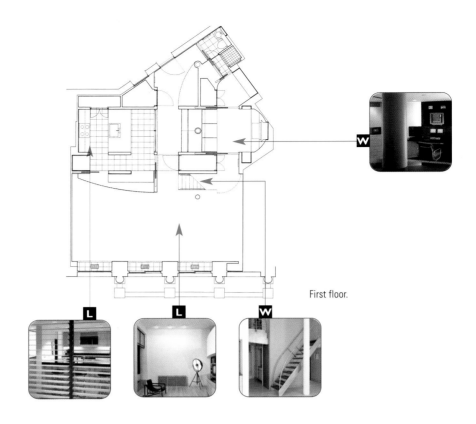

First floor.

AN APARTMENT FOR TWO EXECUTIVES   Frank Lupo and Daniel Rowen

Because of dissatisfaction with their daily commutes to work, many professionals have decided to set up work space at home. The information technology revolution has accelerated this trend. Although the clients for this project have not abandoned their old workplace, they do want to remain on top of things while at home.

The Lipschutz-Jones apartment, located in Lower Manhattan, was designed for a pair of Wall Street stockbrokers. The clients desired flexible, open living space with a work area, essentially a room to house sophisticated computer and communication systems so they could monitor the market at any time. The office had to be easily seen from various locations in the apartment, yet sufficiently isolated so that it did not interfere with day-to-day life.

Two levels at the back, next to the wall forming the building's internal corridor, accommodate the essential activities. At the front, bathed in intense light flooding through floor-to-ceiling windows overlooking the city, there is a two-story living room. A high, narrow passage connects the rooms and partitions off different areas. The kitchen is on one side, with a bedroom above it; the office sits on the other side, below the master bath. This means that the work area is separated from the bedroom but can be seen from the kitchen and central corridor. Along with the office computers, six screens are interspersed throughout the apartment so its residents can keep abreast of international exchanges around the clock.

Access to the upper floor is by a steel staircase. A beam reduces the impact of the bare space created by the corridor, and doubles as a bookcase. From the landing, one can marvel at the magnificent cityscape through the expansive windows. Due to the advantageous location of the living room, there are magnificent views of the façades of the nearby buildings. The floors were singled out for special treatment, so the architects used the best materials. In the rest of the home, a wide palette, including maple wood, marble, granite, and translucent glass, was employed to give the project strong visual character.

View of the living room
showing one of the six screens.

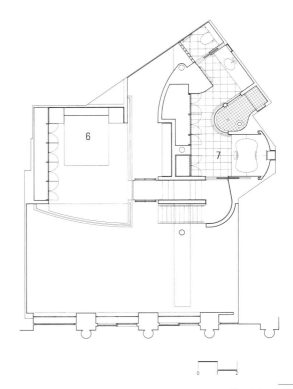

1. Entrance
2. Living room
3. Kitchen
4. Multimedia room
5. Double-height passageway
6. Bedroom
7. Bathroom

Top right: detail of the office.
Bottom right: views of the entrance, the stairs and the bridge that connects the bedroom and the bathroom.
Bottom: the screen on the living room.

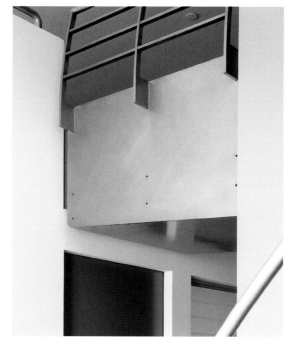

Construction details, such as those on the shower enclosures and the landing banister, were carefully designed. Ceramic, stainless steel, and glass were used in the bathroom.

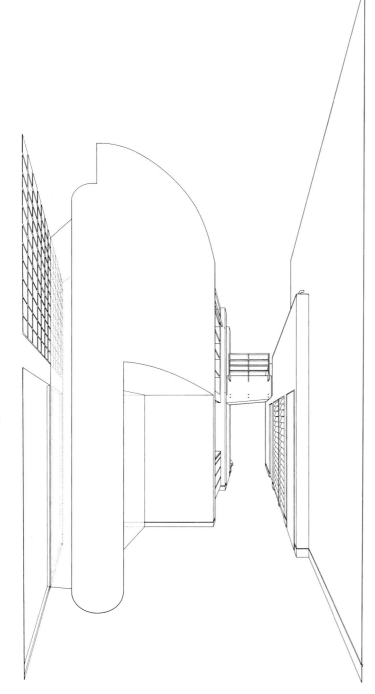

This perspective shows the double height in the apartment.
An ample, flexible space has been partitioned with highly visual, panelled walls.

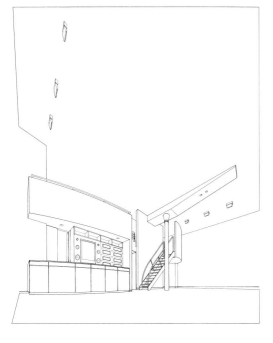

The perspective from the interior

From the onset, the principal objective was to connect the rooms of the home while maintaining acoustic privacy so different activities could be carried out simultaneously.

Top right: view of the kitchen from the outside. Above: six screens where the owners can read the international exchanges are distributed through the apartment: the screen in the bathroom.

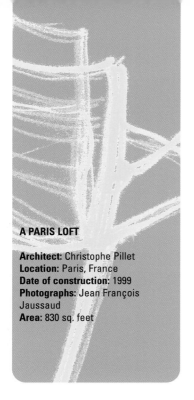

A PARIS LOFT

Architect: Christophe Pillet
Location: Paris, France
Date of construction: 1999
Photographs: Jean François Jaussaud
Area: 830 sq. feet

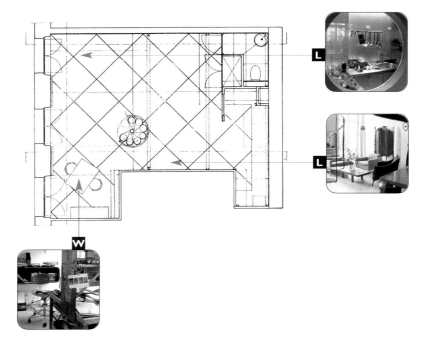

The emergence of new specialized tasks which can be performed outside the office has enabled many professionals to do freelance work from their own homes for several different firms simultaneously. The client who commissioned this project, a design specialist, decided to establish his operating base at home. The dwelling is on two levels: the daytime areas (kitchen, dining room, toilet, studio, and living room, which extends to the second level) are downstairs, while the bedroom with its private bath is upstairs. The connecting iron staircase is twisted like a snail's shell and the stairs, welded to the banister, are petal-shaped (see drawing plans).

The designer tried to connect all the rooms visually to provide a sensation of spaciousness in a home that is really quite small. In addition, since only one wall is external, it was essential that as much light as possible reach the innermost areas of the home. To this end, the vertical partitions which close off the bathroom and bedroom, as well as kitchen and dinning room, include a circular glass window. Another characteristic adding to this sense of roomy comfort is the transparent portion of the upstairs floor, which visually connects all parts of the house.

The client's passion for works of art and designer furniture prompted Christophe Pillet to design a neutral space where functional and decorative elements stand out and take on a special role.

Consequently, unembellished finishes were chosen, such as the gray stone floor and plaster on the walls, and similar shades were used in painting the walls.

The overall effect is an ingeniously distributed, functional, and flexible living space, suitable for the users' domestic and professional activities.

The refinements are understated, but the vivid tones of the furniture and other decorative objects produce a warm, vibrant environment.

The living room.

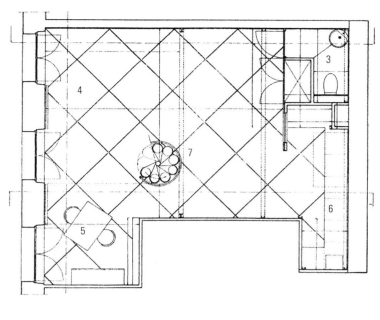

Lower floor

Loft

1. Bedroom
2. Bathroom
3. Toilet
4. Living room
5. Studio
6. Kitchen
7. Petal-shaped staircase

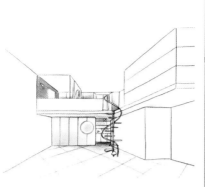

Right: the studio occupies a small corner of the lower floor. Books, prototypes, and drawings are piled on shelves, creating an inspiring atmosphere for the client, an industrial design specialist. Left: the dinning room and the small kitchen are connected through a circular window.

Top: the living room.
Bottom: the bedroom. The
limited size of the project was
the reason Christophe Pillet
designed connected spaces,
like the bathroom and
bedroom, which have openings
in their walls to maintain a
visual relationship with the
other rooms in the home.

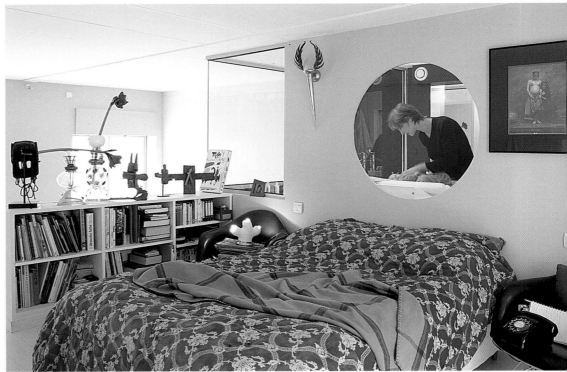

Top left: This window visually connects living room with kitchen.

Top: to emphasize the perceptual relationship among areas, some of the loft flooring is transparent, providing a view of the kitchen.

Left: detail of the baby's bedroom.

A HOUSE IN LA CLOTA

Architects: Enric Miralles and Benedetta Tagliabue
Collborator: Josep Ustrell
Location: Barcelona, Spain
Date of onstruction: 1998
Photographs: Jordi Miralles
Area: 2,080 sq. feet

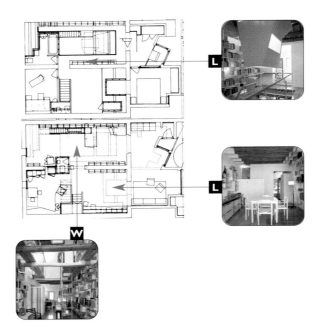

I HOUSE + I HOUSE = I ROOM   Enric Miralles and Benedetta Tagliabue

This project joined two houses in Barcelona's La Clota neighborhood, restoring, expanding, and converting them into a unique home, with a studio-library playing a key role. The general structure of the first building was preserved. The living room, dining room, and, the kitchen, at the back, remain along with the three second floor bedrooms. The staircase was retained and beams were exposed in some rooms.

The changes to the other house were more drastic. The center was gutted and a walkway and skylight were installed, the latter filling the interior with light. The varied shades of white paint and the different woods in the flooring enhance this luminosity.

This part of the project includes an entrance hall which opens onto a living area, both created by extending the building and a two-story library. The wooden beams are partly painted white. Bookcases cover the walls, and a walkway provides access to the higher shelves and leading to the bathroom in the other wing. The walkway is interrupted by a pine platform, adjacent to the bedroom, which can be used as a quiet reading corner or an improvised dressing room.

Access to the upper floor is by the old staircase or the new one located next to the desk area. This light staircase is movable and includes shelves. It perfectly matches the style of the home because, like most of the furnishings, it was designed by the architects themselves.

One of the project's principal objectives was to preserve the building's original feel, and ceilings, walls, beams, and certain fragments of previous paint layers were left exposed. The façade had to take into consideration the somewhat chaotic character of the La Clota buildings. Mortar and natural brick were chosen so the house would blend in. The front door is made of aluminum.

View of the two-story library and the movable staircase.

The working space
from the back of the
house.

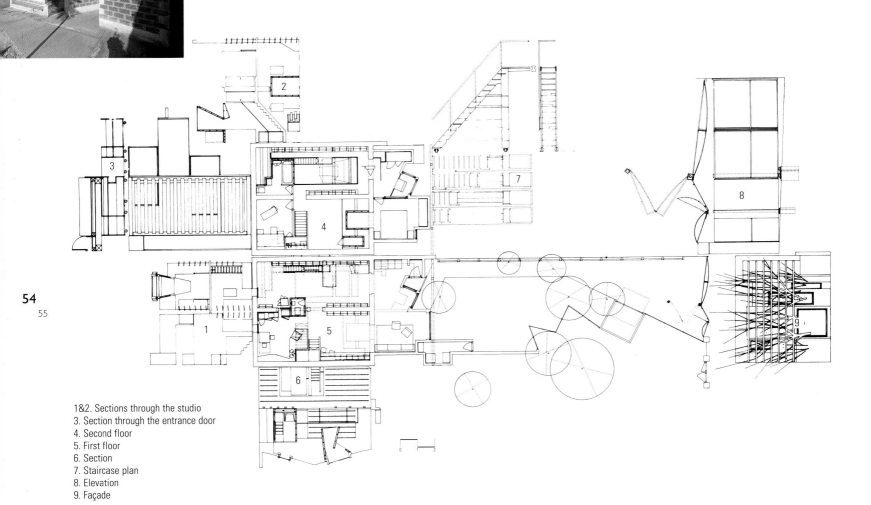

1&2. Sections through the studio
3. Section through the entrance door
4. Second floor
5. First floor
6. Section
7. Staircase plan
8. Elevation
9. Façade

Sketches of the skylight that
illuminates the library.

Right: walkways were devised to reach all the library shelves and provide a connection to the bathroom.

Bottom right: the skylight was designed so light would filter down to the first floor of the home. An opening in one of the skylight covers allows light to enter the library.

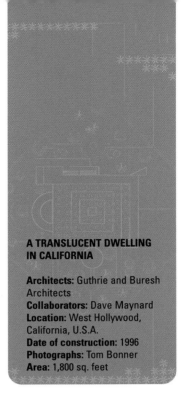

A TRANSLUCENT DWELLING IN CALIFORNIA

Architects: Guthrie and Buresh Architects
Collaborators: Dave Maynard
Location: West Hollywood, California, U.S.A.
Date of construction: 1996
Photographs: Tom Bonner
Area: 1,800 sq. feet

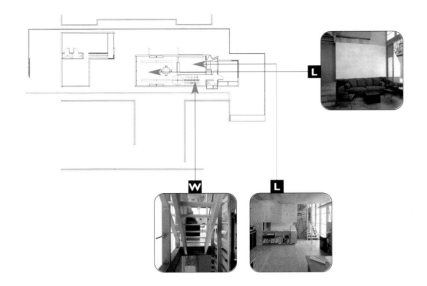

A HOUSE AND WORKSHOP FOR ARCHITECTS   Guthrie and Buresh Architects

Designed by Danelle Guthrie and Tom Buresh to be both their residence and workplace, this house is in West Hollywood, a residential area of Los Angeles that started out as a working class neighborhood. A small structure still stands on the front part of the site, blocking the noise from the busy street that runs by. Eventually, this small building will be replaced by a house/studio available for rent.

The project involved a three-story wooden building with living room, kitchen, and covered parking on the first level, and the studio and children's bedroom on the second floor. Above are the master bedroom and a terrace or sun deck.

Two materials are predominant in the house: wooden planks for the floors and walls, and polycarbonate panels for the façade. The translucent quality of the façade produces what the architects describe as "a state of continuous flux that depends on the light intensity at each moment and the position of the observer." The arrangement communicates Guthrie and Buresh's ideas about the powerful relationship, the mutual consideration, that should exist between private and public spaces in densely populated areas. They go even further and assert that spaces shared visually by two side-by-side buildings challenge the psychological impenetrability of property lines, while the translucent membrane of the front provides needed intimacy.

Inside, the living areas are separated from the workshop with variations in levels, strategic placement of panels, and overlapping, intermediate spaces. The building itself is influenced by landmark projects in the area.

The way the translucent panels close off the space brings to mind the light façade of the Eames House, while developing low-cost techniques recalls Rudolph Schindler's house.

The house and worshop
from the outside.

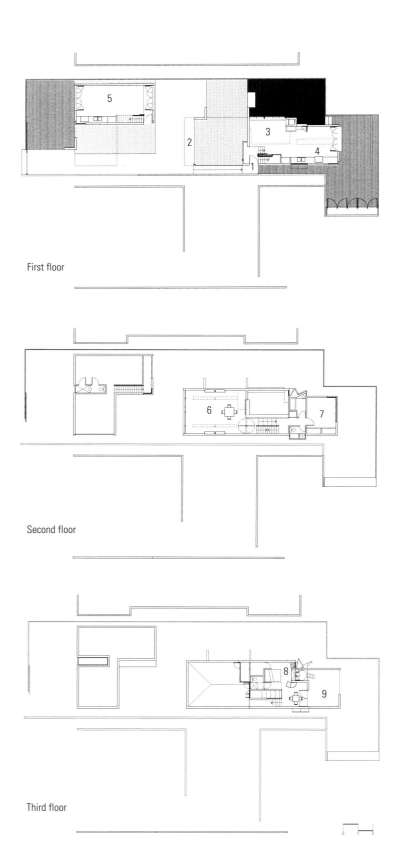

First floor

Second floor

Third floor

1. Entrance
2. Garage
3. Living room
4. Kitchen/dining room
5. Empty space for future building
6. Work space
7. Bedroom
8. Main bedroom
9. Terrace

The exterior views show the translucent and opaque facades of the project that melts into the neighbourhood thanks to its form and to the surrounding vegetation.

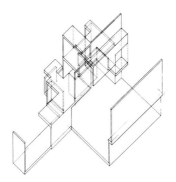

Axonometric perspectives.

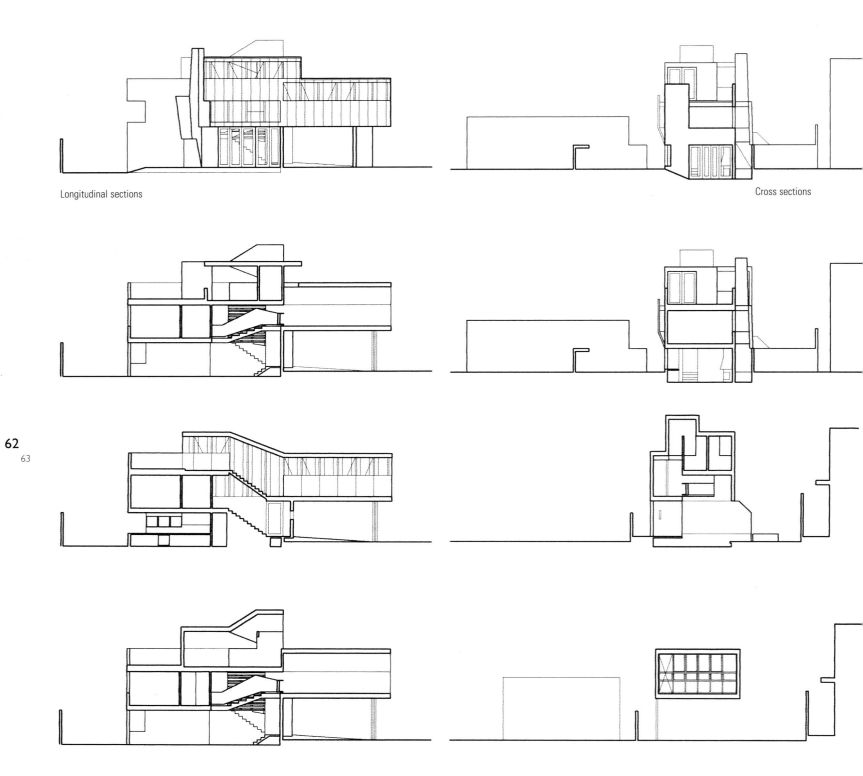

Longitudinal sections

Cross sections

The floor and walls use plywood. The translucent polycarbonate façade permits an intelligent relationship between the interior and exterior.

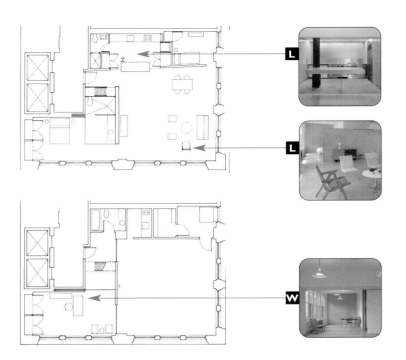

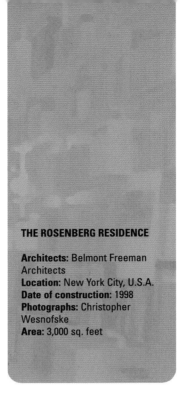

THE ROSENBERG RESIDENCE

Architects: Belmont Freeman
Architects
Location: New York City, U.S.A.
Date of construction: 1998
Photographs: Christopher
Wesnofske
Area: 3,000 sq. feet

A DUAL LOFT IN MANHATTAN   Belmont Freeman Architects

Living and working in the same place offers undeniable advantages in terms of one's schedule, and enjoying the privilege of doing one's professional work in a pleasant, family environment. The Rosenberg residence, in an early 20th Century commercial building in lower Manhattan, converted to living space during the 1980s, has made the most of this functional duality. The decision to place the dwelling and studio on different levels has enabled the users to enjoy specific, distinct environments in the same apartment.

The project involves two 1,500-square-foot floors, vertically connected, with the interior renovated as an office, studio, and home for an art-loving resident. The relationship between the two units played a prominent role, with the architects developing a plan which joins both parts while allowing them independence.

On the upper floor the dwelling contains a living room, a kitchen, and two bedrooms. No partition breaks up the exterior wall, which admits generous light from the north. The lower level, with its restored, sandblasted concrete flooring covered in zinc casting, serves as an office and studio.

Two mobile screens, one of plasterboard and the other of translucent glass, make it easy to rearrange the apartment. The two levels are connected by a staircase which seems to have come straight from a ship and which separates the work area and the living area on the upper floor.

A strict, controlled palette of materials (concrete, maple, stainless steel and laminated glass) has forged a space with simple yet elegant finishes. Some elements, such as the bathroom and the work top in the kitchen, were designed by the architects themselves. The owner also contributed to the refined aesthetics with a magnificent collection of modern furniture.

View of the upper floor. It contains the bedroom, kitchen and living room.

The project is located in a commercial building dating from the early 1900s, which was converted into a residential complex in the eighties.

First and second floors
1. Kitchen
2. Bedroom
3. Bedroom
4. Bathroom
5. Living room
6. Dining room
7. Office
8. Studio

0   1   2

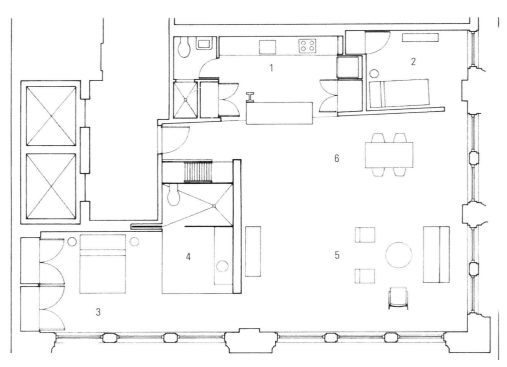

First floor

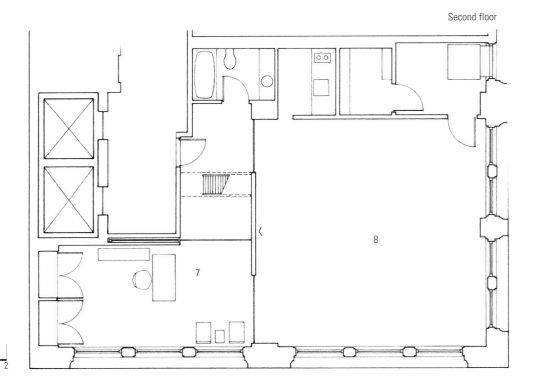

Second floor

The stairs, typical of ships, connect the two levels and separate the work area from the private quarters on the upper floor.

The special relationship between the two levels is a key element of the project.

The lower level,
with an original
surface, has
been set aside
for the office and
work studio.

On the right, views of the
bathroom and kitchen,
both with furnishings
designed exclusively for
the project.

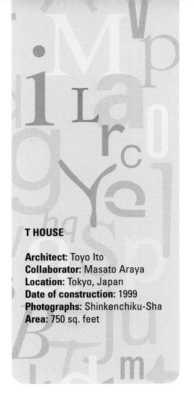

T HOUSE

Architect: Toyo Ito
Collaborator: Masato Araya
Location: Tokyo, Japan
Date of construction: 1999
Photographs: Shinkenchiku-Sha
Area: 750 sq. feet

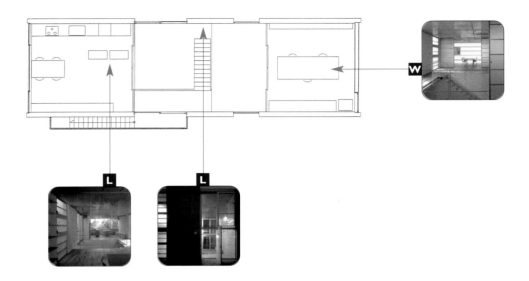

HOUSE FOR TWO GRAPHIC DESIGNERS   Toyo Ito

oyo Ito uses strategies such as transparency and the superimposition of distinct planes, along with persistent references to virtual reality and the world of communications and information technology. This creates a fresh architecture, expounding the new spirit of the times, which in this project allows the clients, two graphic designers and their independent businessman son, to work from home.

Although the house is in an urban area, a large window at the back offers exhilarating views of the lush neighboring garden. The residents spend most of their time at home, where professional and private activities take place side-by-side without a clear dividing line. The design is based on a life concept which embraces discrete, heterogeneous spaces. The studio, bedrooms, and bathrooms are laid out in parallel.

The architecture and variety of materials were played down and adapted to accommodate the three individuals' privacy needs. The layout includes three modules linked by empty spaces from the ground floor to the roof. This gives the house the feeling of being a whole and not a mere succession of rooms, fitting in perfectly with the relationships among the inhabitants, close but independent.

Although committed to his guiding principles, the architect from the first intended to create a comfortable home, satisfying the clients' needs and requirements with simple mechanical construction elements, to take advantage of natural phenomena such as the breeze, the sunlight and the relationship with the neighborhood.

View of the main entrance.

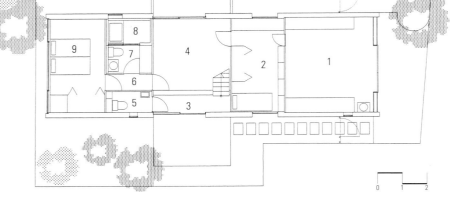

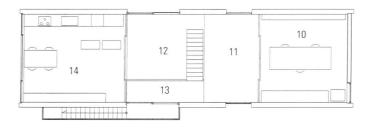

1. Garage
2. Bedroom
3. Entrance
4. Foyer
5. Toilet
6. Passage
7. Bathroom
8. Bathroom
9. Main bedroom
10. Office
11. Office
12. Empty space
13. Bridge
14. Living room

View of the exterior facade at night. The concrete facade constrasts with the transparent glass panels of the entrance and the translucent windows.

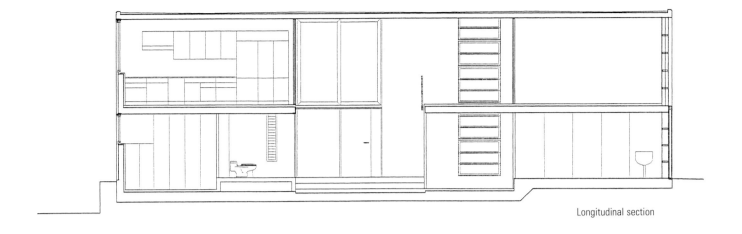

Longitudinal section

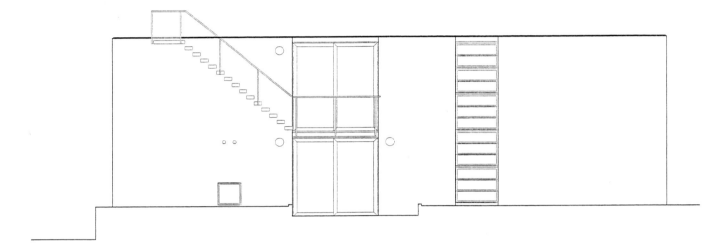

South elevation

East elevation

The house is constructed in an urban area.

The upper floor locates the working areas.

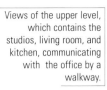
Views of the upper level, which contains the studios, living room, and kitchen, communicating with the office by a walkway.

Close-up of the translucent panels on the façade and some of the interior panels. The strict arrangement balances the building's components.

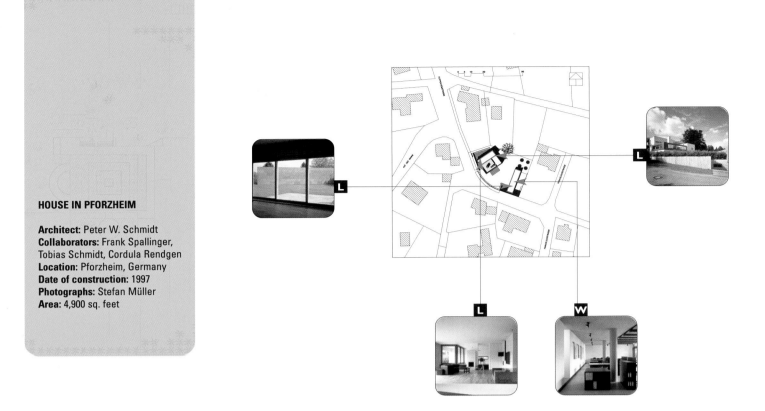

HOUSE IN PFORZHEIM

Architect: Peter W. Schmidt
Collaborators: Frank Spallinger,
Tobias Schmidt, Cordula Rendgen
Location: Pforzheim, Germany
Date of construction: 1997
Photographs: Stefan Müller
Area: 4,900 sq. feet

AN ARCHITECT'S HOME AND STUDIO   Peter W. Schmidt

ll architects want to design their own home, giving free reign to their desires and caprices. This also gives them the opportunity to implement ideas they would not dare try with other clients. It is the perfect chance to experiment and devise new solutions. This project consisted of a home and studio on high ground overlooking the German town of Pforzheim. Peter W. Schmidt made the decision to live and work in the same place to avoid the hassle of the daily commute to the office.

The functional organization of the complex respects the independence of the two structures, although they are connected by their strategic placement on the site. Each has a patio, but the rugged ground is common to both. A garden was created by leveling off the slope.

Although the structures are physically separate, the use of the same materials and construction details provides uniformity. Reinforced concrete is covered by stone. Sliding doors and windows framed in cedar give a feeling of openness. The flooring varies. In the living areas, smooth, gray beechwood is used in the living room and entrance hall. Stone was laid down in the kitchen, and alluring terra-cotta mosaics add tasteful touches to the bathroom. The service area and passages utilize non-porous, epoxy resin ceramics. There is no need to be notable just to be noticed, so this special project has a conventional layout: the common areas are on the first floor and the more private rooms are upstairs, opening onto a balcony. The building housing the architect's studio has rigid proportions. It is a large room with direct access to the garden.

The reinforced concrete structure is covered by basalt slabs outside and plaster inside. Large windows allow intense light, so important for work, to enter. The unhindered views provide a feeling of continuity and accentuate the relationship with the outside.

The building consists of two
independent structures.

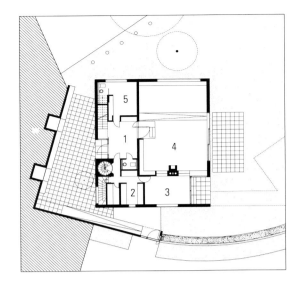

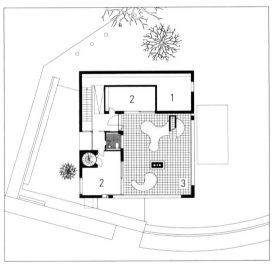

First floor

1. Entrance
2. Kitchen
3. Dining room
4. Living room
5. Guest bedroom

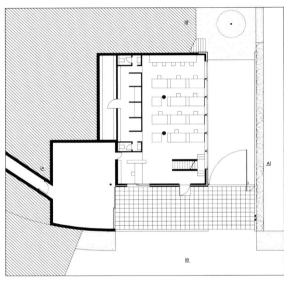

Second floor

1. Library
2. Children's bedroom
3. Balcony

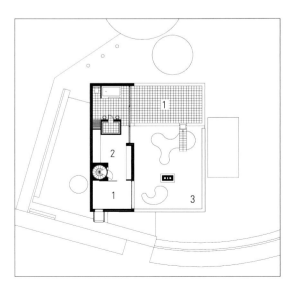

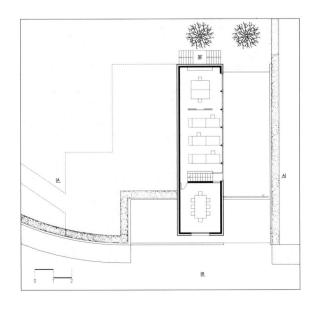

Third floor

1. Main bedroom
2. Dressing room
3. Balcony
4. Studio

0 1 2

The exterior has been carefully planned to intensify the very close relationship with the interior through a surrounding passageway. Views include the building's stone walls and the garden, with grass, lush bushes, and a few trees.

South elevation

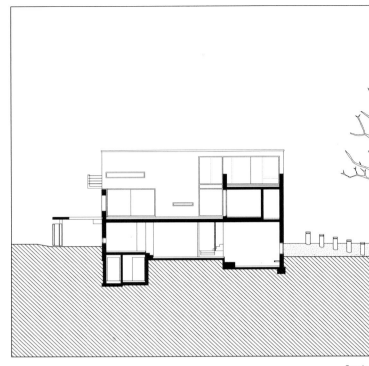

Section

East elevation

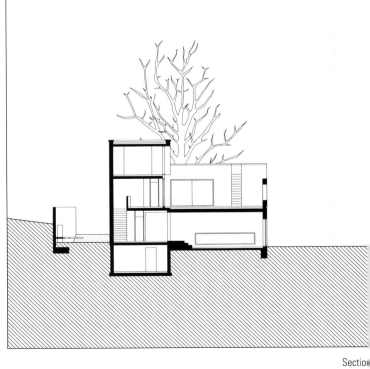

Section

The studio is a large, non-compartmentalized room opening onto the garden through the entirely glass front. The woodwork, an abstract, geometric composition, flows from room to room.

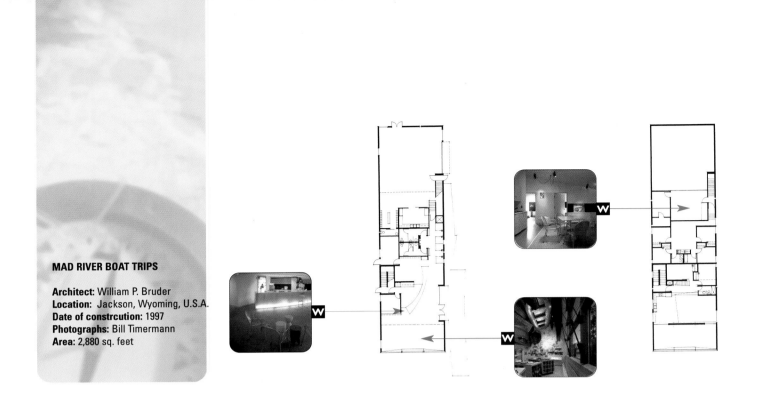

MAD RIVER BOAT TRIPS

Architect: William P. Bruder
Location: Jackson, Wyoming, U.S.A.
Date of constrcution: 1997
Photographs: Bill Timermann
Area: 2,880 sq. feet

A SHOP-MUSEUM, WAREHOUSE, AND HOME FOR ADVENTURERS   William P. Bruder

Because of the particular complexity of this project, a building with three functions, the layout had to be exacting. Connections had to be simple. Private and public areas could not to be mixed.

The warehouse for the boats and special equipment, such as waterproof clothing, ropes, and tools, has a small section for serving customers. Clients are welcomed into the shop through a reception area where they can relax and admire imaginative touches, such as a sculpted counter made from translucent fiber-cement accented by green and blue spotlights, evoking the waves and ripples of a river. It is an ideal environment for selling products, souvenirs, books, and videos related to rafting and other outdoor activities. The public space includes a museum with information about the region, its traditions and folklore. Maps, photos, and texts are displayed, while antique boats and other items bring the past vividly into focus. The museum enjoys commanding views of the waterfall behind the building, typical of the wild beauty of this western, paradisaical state.

The private areas are divided into rooms for the workers and a residence for the owner, with a library and studio. The guides' and drivers' accommodations had to comply with labor law regulations. The tight budget was another factor. The guest rooms above the shop and museum are somewhat more elegant. Despite the considerable functional diversity, the architect produced a logical, compact layout.

Simple wood construction techniques were used for the building.

The upper levels are suspended from a beam arrangement, which permits greater flexibility for the first floor. Two special wood and steel beams hold the east-facing glass façade in place. The roof and walls employ corrugated iron, making for a rugged appearance; windows are arranged to achieve a rhythmic composition both day and night.

Building systems play an important role in this type of architecture. Bruder selected built-in heaters and ventilation through versatile windows and shutters. Air-conditioning and, sometimes, a fan reduce humidity in a climate that can be extreme.

The lighting design is highly efficient in the work area and dramatic in the shop and museum.

The headquarters of Mad River Boat Trips evokes the traditional ranches nearby. At the same time, it is a landmark which stands out in the ambiguous area along the interstate highway. The building is a robust, sophisticated architectural expression of the strength of the individuals who delight in the nature of Wyoming.

Mad River Boat Trips is located in the magnificent surroundings of Wyoming.

Different views of the building façade. The interior photo shows the part of the shop in which rafting-related products are sold.

Third floor

Second floor

First floor

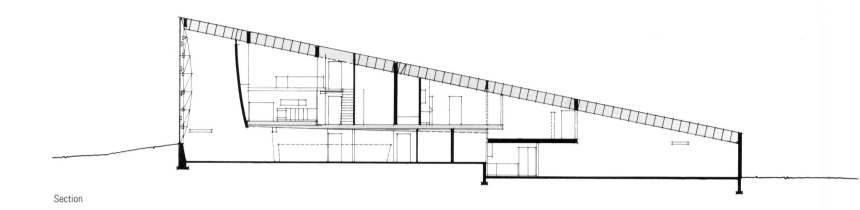

Section

The Mad River Boat Trips complex is evocative of the region's typical ranches and recalls Wyoming's pioneering roots. Its simple elegance commands attention in the undefined zone next to the interstate highway which cuts through the commercial area.
Left: view of the dressing room.
Right: the warehouse.

The lighting was designed to be highly efficient in the work areas and to create dramatic effects in the shop and the museum, as for example, the counter on the reception that includes color spotlights.

Below, close-up of the stairs leading to the owner's living areas. On the left, stairs connecting the living room with the loft bedroom.

The living room wall includes windows of various sizes that admit natural light while creating an energetic, rhythmic composition on the outside.

CONVERTING A BLACKSMITH SHOP

Architects: Sergi Bastidas, B&B Architecture studio
Location: Palma de Mallorca, Spain
Date of construction: 1999
Photographs: Pere Planells
Area: 3,600 sq. feet

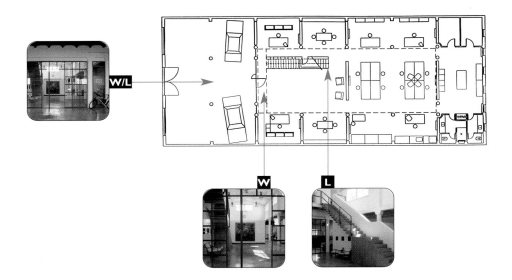

AN ARCHITECT'S HOME AND STUDIO   Sergi Bastidas, B&B Architecture Studio

This former smithy, converted into a studio and home for an architect, is in Molinar, a small village on the island of Majorca. The guiding principle from the beginning was to maintain the blacksmith's ample, open work space.

The first decision was to install transparent glass in slender wooden frames to demarcate the entrance hall, providing a first visual impression of spaciousness and emphasizing the brightness and industrial associations of the project. The space was divided by less-than-ceiling-height plaster panels, to preserve the expansive, unified feeling. These panels differentiate the various areas of the first floor and are ideal for hanging pictures. On the upper floor, sliding vertical partitions separate the living areas from the meeting room.

Out of respect for the building's original industrial nature, the designers chose simple lines, untreated finishes, and rough materials such as polished concrete for the floor. They retained the existing mechanical structures. The ceiling trusses, double window frame, and columns were also preserved. Some of the decorative objects, including the lamps hanging from the ceiling, also conjure up the building's past.

The second floor emphasizes intimacy and privacy, with functional spatial division. The bathroom's specially designed furnishings set off a circular shower as the core element. The stone cylinder does not reach the ceiling, so full advantage can be taken of the light entering the room. The stairs, with steps cut out of a concrete slab, were also designed specifically for the project. This sculptural yet functional feature harmonizes effectively with the other elements.

There is a visual connection between the working spaces and the living areas located on the upper floor.

The exterior clearly shows the industrial character of the original building. This factory ambience was preserved by creating transparent, open, flexible space.

View from the entrance. On the left, the staircase leading to the upper floor.

The staircase is like a sculpture in concrete which opens to form the steps.

Top: view of the little kitchen, the bathroom doors and dining room for the workers of the architectural atelier. Bottom: detail of the stainless steel kitchen.

The office is separated from the other rooms by a partition that does not reach the ceiling. This mechanism has been used frequently because it permits an overall appreciation of the project and maintains functionality.

1. Meeting room
2. Private bathroom
3. Bedroom
4. Living room
5. Empty space from first floor space
6. Garage
7. Entrance
8. Studio
9. Toilets
10. Office

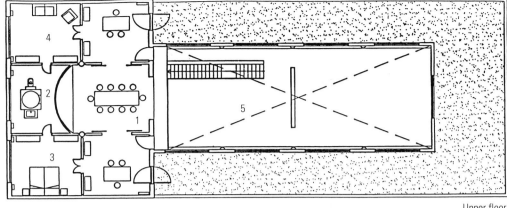

Upper floor

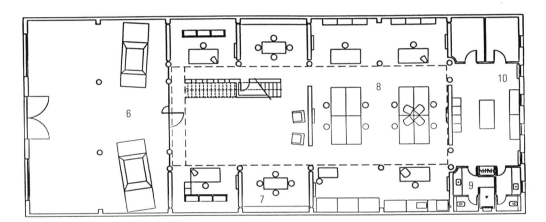

Lower floor

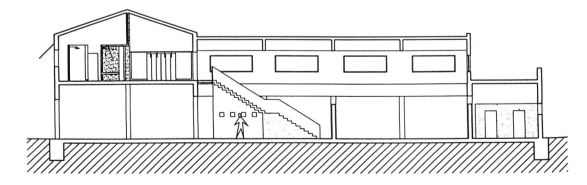

The meeting room, although it adjoins the double-height space and lacks doors, has an intimate feel and remains separate from the studio.

The upper floor includes the residence and meeting room. This floor is the most clearly delineated area, where the rooms have specific, rather than interchangeable, functions. It locates a bathroom and a dressing room.

A HOUSE STUDIO IN STOCKHOLM

Architects: Jacques Sandjian,
Claesson Koivisto Rune Architects
Collaborators: Deta Gemzell and
Stephanie Sacher
Location: Stockholm, Sweden
Date of construction: 1998
Photographs: Åke E:son Lindman
Area: 1,660 sq. feet

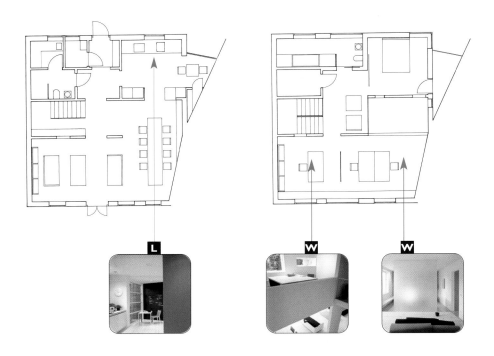

HOME FOR A TEXTILE DESIGNER   Claesson Koivisto Rune Architects

This dwelling on a hill near Stockholm served as the prototype for a fifty-unit, mixed residential project by a large Swedish property developer. Architect Jacques Sandjian was commissioned to do the exterior work, while a team worked on the interior.

Since at the time there was no owner or specific client, the architects decided to have designer Pia Wallén serve as a typical client to help them develop the plan. Wallén was selected because the architects, with whom she had worked previously, felt she shared their interest in the abstract values of architecture, such as space, light, visual perspective, and flexibility.

The house, on two levels, has a dining room, kitchen, bedroom, two bathrooms, dressing room, and a generous area for the studio and office. In spatial terms, the architects envisioned a duplex with a large, open vertical section containing a staircase and a two-story central area, pervaded by light. The project focused on eliminating dividers and doors to emphasize visual interconnection. The partitions create a rich pattern of planes and volumes and give the project a dynamic edge.

Wood is the key material throughout the home. The floor is made of oak with a white varnish, even in the kitchen. Larch is used on the terrace. The furniture, designed by the architects, is pine, except for the bathroom pieces, which are made of larch because of its waterproof qualities.

The other eye-catching feature of the project is color. Although the predominant tone on the doors and walls is white, gray panels accent the staircase, while red is used in the entrance hall and slate in the office area. These colors can be seen from any corner of the home through the many openings in the partitions.

View of the studio on the upper floor. The atelier is divided in two by a glazed partition.

The vertical partitions have unexpected breaks or small openings which connect the areas of the house.

Left page: view of the double story space from the upper floor.

Bottom: the two-story space around the stairs deepens the intense visual connection.

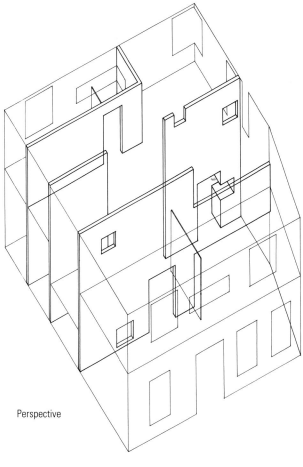

Perspective

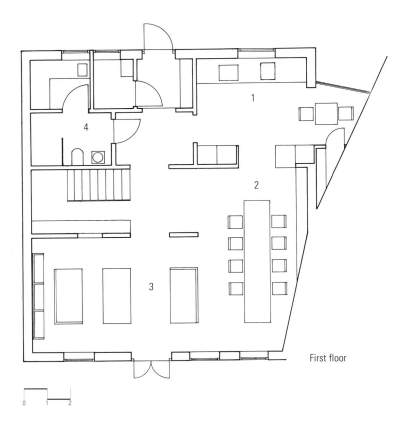

1. Kitchen
2. Dining room
3. Living room
4. Toilet
5. Bedroom
6. Free space
7. Studio
8. Bathroom

First floor

0   1   2

Second floor

The house is full of ingenious solutions which ensure a practical and comfortable home life. The slate kitchen wall provides a decorative detail.

Wood dominates throughout the building. Different types were used according to their strength, durability, and resistance to water and insects.

Because of the close relationship between the architects and their textile designer client, fabrics in a variety of colors cover most of the furniture.

The studio is divided in two. Above: detail of the table were the textile designer works. The other part of the atelier is used as an office.

The true luxury of the project stems from its luminosity and spaciousness, rather than the decorative objects. Moreover, the harmoniousness of the building gives serenity to the entire project.

The bath is also made of wood, specifically larch, because of its water-resistant properties. Grey ceramic was used to accentuate one bathroom partition.

Two views of the upper floor. Before entering the bedroom, there is a small hall overlooking the first floor.

**CHRISTOPHE PILLET
APARTMENT**

Architect: Christophe Pillet
Location: Paris, France
Date of construction: 1999
Photographs: Agence Omnia
Area: 1,350 sq. feet

A DESIGNER'S HOME AND STUDIO   Christophe Pillet

When not working for prestigious international firms, French designer Christophe Pillet does interior decoration, creating ideas for shops, hotels, showrooms, and homes. He planned his Paris residence, a home with a studio, next to the historic Père Lachaise cemetery. This renovation can be considered as a remodelling more than a new architectural work. It consisted of three simple steps: taking out as many walls as possible to provide as much space as possible, cleaning and preserving the structure, and painting everything white. This resulted in an austere environment with key roles being played by the emptiness, the light that floods the home through the many large windows, and the two immense skylights over the living area. The dwelling revolves around two principal spaces: the living room/dining room and, on another level, the two-room studio. In the former, the original beams are exposed, painted the same color as the walls.

The studio was decorated with the same simplicity that Pillet imposed on the living area. His work space is an L-shaped table against the wall with an easel opposite. The original woodwork of the window frames, painted white, the radiator system with bare pipes, and the wooden dais have been preserved.

Emphasizing frugality and moderation, Pillet has created a flexible environment suitable for the select pieces of design furniture that have been introduced. There are Eames chairs and many other pieces by celebrated designers, but most of the furniture consists of his own design prototypes that have been sent to him for testing. He likes a fresh ambience and does not want to be surrounded by the same objects all the time, so he enjoys changing the prototypes every time something new arrives.

The living room is a mixture of classical designs and prototypes by the owner.

In the home of the prestigious French designer, a neutral, flexible atmosphere predominates, ideal for accommodating many contrasting design elements: most are prototypes created by the owner himself.
Left: main entrance with a stair leading to the living room.

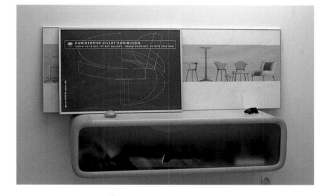

Christophe Pillet remembers the great masters. His living room contains a table by Arne Jacobsen and chairs by Charles and Ray Eames.
Bottom center: view of one of the living room's corner.
Bottom right: the entrance to the bedroom.

The working space.

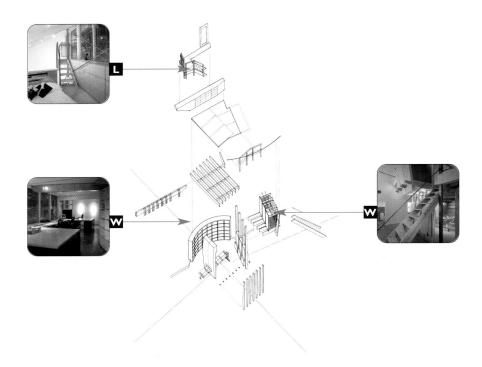

**AN ECOLOGICAL HOME
AND STUDIO**

Architect: Randy Brown
Collaborators: Tom Allisma,
Cynthia Ray, Christian Petrick and
Jason Winterboer
Location: Omaha, Nebraska, U.S.A.
Date of construction: 1997
Photographs: Farshid Assassi
Area: 1,725 sq. feet

rchitect Randy Brown decided to locate his studio-residence in a former nursery school which had been abandoned in 1970. He was eager to test himself with a piece of experimental architecture and was looking for an adventure in which he could depart from the norm and feel free to go off on a tangent. He did not set out just to create a home. Part of his game plan was to live through the changes, the progress from four walls on the grounds of an estate to a completed project. So he and his wife moved in when nothing but the bathroom was ready.

He gutted the interior, analyzed what he could convert the shell into, and set up and removed elements in a trial-and-error process until he had a building appropriate to his lifestyle and philosophy, and which could accommodate his work rituals.

His creed includes a commitment to ecology and a willingness to take chances. He applied these to the multifaceted problem of energy sources for building construction, maintenance, and operation. In the United States, buildings consume about 45% of all energy. Resource-conserving architecture can create a house which is powered by sun, wind, and flowing water. Simple design adjustments (such as orientation to the sun, solar power, and using recycled materials) can reduce consumption by up to 75%.

The building has two stories. The studio and living areas are on the first floor, with the bedroom and dressing room upstairs. Downstairs, the architect marked out three areas. The studio is on one side, the dining room and conference room are in the middle, and the kitchen and bath, with space for the photocopier, are on the other side.

The conference room contains the most representative piece of design furniture in the home: a pine framework with steel-plate laminate, the lower part of which adjoins the dining room table and the upper part of which forms the headboard of the bed in the second floor bedroom.

The pine structure has a curved steel veneer. The upper part is the headboard of the bed and the lower part is connected to the dining room table.

The home's glass façade guarantees natural light and connection with the garden. Right: view of the wooden stairs that lead to the private area of the house.

1. Kitchen
2. Bathroom
3. Studio
4. Conference room
5. Bedroom
6. Terrace

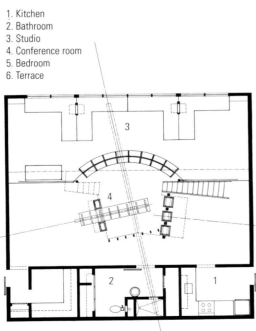

First floor

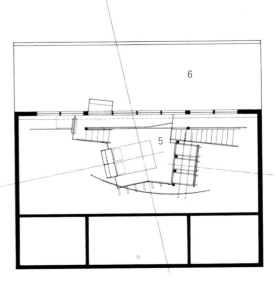

Second floor

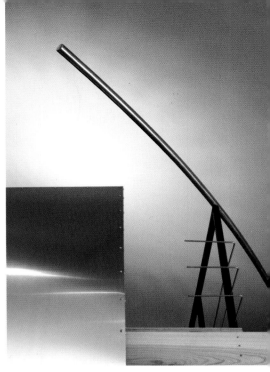

All construction elements (stairs, banisters, and balconies) were designed by the architect, mainly using wood and stainless steel.

The main bedroom, on the second floor, enjoys a magnificent panoramic view of the landscape.
It also directly accesses an enormous terrace on top of the studio.

View of the upper part of the curved veneer. It is used as the headboard of the bed.

Staircase from office to bedroom.

Bedroom.

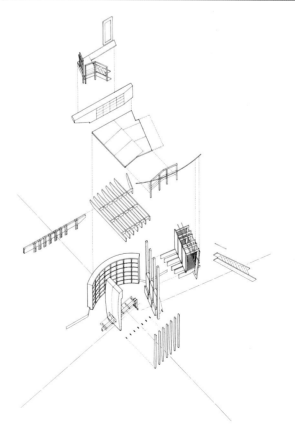

The studio furniture is also Brown's work. Here, some of the walls have been left bare so they can be used to exhibit his projects.

Top right: view of the bathroom and the kitchen. Both were built using recycled materials.

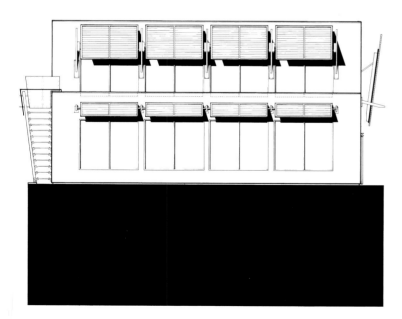

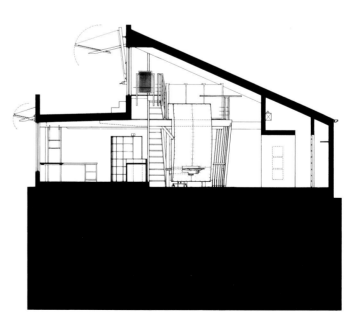

Rear façade

Cross section

ISOBE STUDIO HOUSE

Architect: Shinichi Ogawa
Location: Yamaguchi, Japan
Date of construction: 1996
Photographs: Shinkenchiku-sha
Area: 1,800 sq. feet

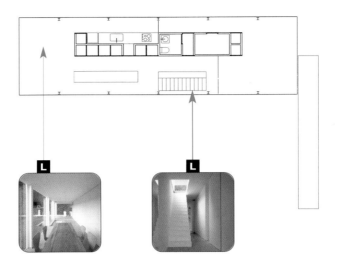

A DESIGNER'S GLASS STUDIO   Shinichi Ogawa

The Isobe studio is near a freeway on the outskirts of the town of Yamaguchi, nestled in a valley surrounded by forested mountains. The steep slope of the site prompted the architect to design a two-story house, the top floor of which is accessed from the road by a concrete bridge.

The space was divided into eight-foot sections. Each square or block became part of the building in a methodical exercise which created a rational and precise conceptual whole.

Areas with the most activity, the living room, kitchen, and work space, are on the upper level, enclosed in a glass frame, 16 feet wide and 57 feet long. In the center, a large white box houses the kitchen, a toilet, and a storage room. The living space, dining room, and studio, in the entrance area, are clearly visible through large panes of glass. The designer deliberately rejected partitions in this area of the house.

The lightness of the upper floor contrasts with the powerful concrete below. The west wall, which runs parallel to the street, has no openings.

All the private areas of the house are on the lower floor: three bedrooms, a bathroom, and a tunnel-like corridor which connects the rooms. In the center, rectangular containers are used as closets.

The interior of the dwelling has been entirely finished in white, even the doors and closets. The flooring is polished concrete on the upper level, with unvarnished wood downstairs. The furniture has been limited to functional pieces in order to maintain flexibility with minimal visual obstruction. The project's character is enhanced by the client's artwork, strategically placed throughout the house and surrounding garden, like a gallery opening out onto the landscape.

Although a markedly geometric structure, the house does not clash with its setting. The simplicity of the finishes makes the project stand out and demonstrates how elegance can be enhanced by natural surroundings.

View of the house in its setting. The graphic designer's studio is located at the entrance of the house.

Perspective

The studio, seen on the right side of the above image, has magnificent views of the surrounding landscape. It is also directly conected with the exterior through a glass door.

The upper floor includes all the common areas. The dining room and living room are visible but the other rooms, such as the kitchen, are concealed inside the central structure of the house.

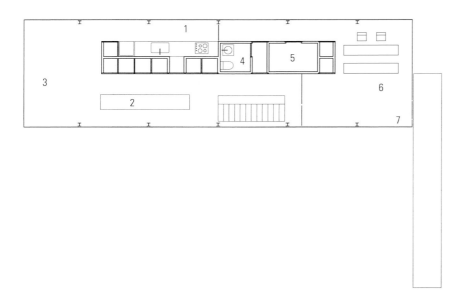

1. Kitchen
2. Dining room
3. Living room
4. Toilet
5. Storage room
6. Studio
7. Entrance
8. Master bedroom
9. Bedrooms
10. Bathroom

The clients of the owner can see the studio from the outside garden as it is the first room of the house. This position keeps the dwelling private and the atelier directly related to the street.

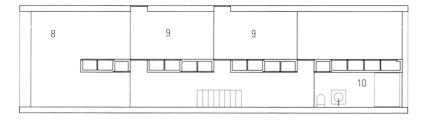

Images on the right show different aspects of the private areas, such as the corridor, one of the bedrooms and the bathroom, all with great views to the garden.

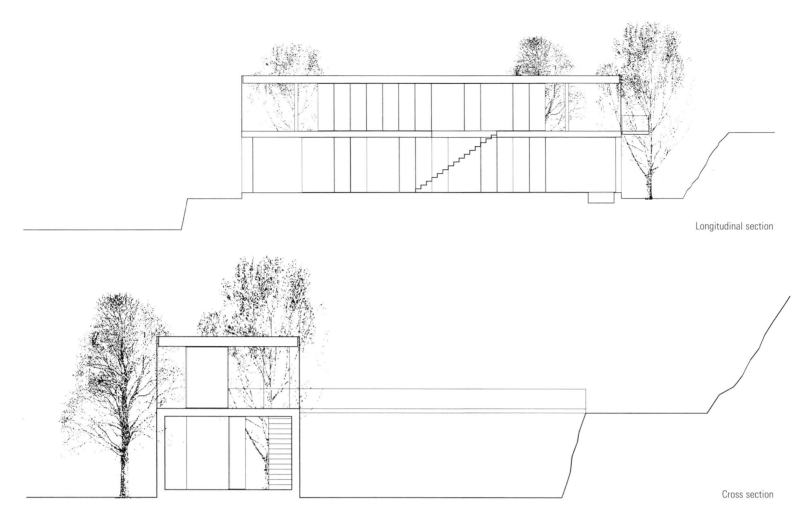

Longitudinal section

Cross section

A HOME AND STUDIO IN ESSEN

Architect: Jürgen Reichardt
Location: Essen, Germany
Date of construction: 1996
Photographs: Klaus Ravenstein
Area: 2,260 sq. feet

First floor   Second floor

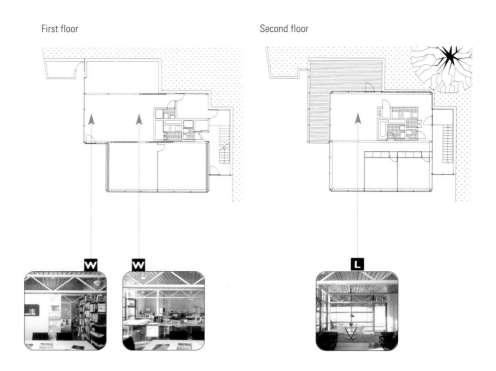

SPACE FOR LIVING AND DESIGNING   Jürgen Reichardt

Architect Jürgen Reichardt built his home and workshop on the site of an old, south-facing coal deposit. The building, slotted into a twenty foot slope, has a reinforced-concrete supporting wall, which provides enough heat insulation to compensate for the delicacy of the building's metal structure.

The flat deck is raised approximately three feet above ground at the back of the house to take advantage of the northern sun's precious rays as they filter through the upper façade. The roof is covered with grass, making the building almost a part of the surrounding terrain.

The project was based on a commitment to keep the building's surface area to a minimum. This was best achieved with a cube, built around the building's nerve center. The entrance and floor-to-floor access are to one side in an annex, which provides a feeling of height and involves a nearby chestnut tree. Another annex forms a terrace on the northeast corner, off the first floor living room.

Since home is where Reichardt works and lives with his family, a compact space was ideal. The office and guest bedroom are on the first floor while the living area is on the second floor. Fluid space in the center interconnects the rooms, while mobile metallic partitions break up the space according to specific requirements.

The diversity of materials makes the building seem a hybrid: the skeleton is metal, the retaining wall is reinforced concrete, the façade is green-covered metal panels, and a reddish wood was used for the windows. The intricate steel detailing was accomplished with prefabricated pieces, all carefully fitted and mounted on a framework.

The trademark of Jürgen Reichardt's work is the special care he gives the environment. His own house could be no exception. He used computer simulations to minimize energy use, and the roof-top solar panels are cutting edge. The house may be a status symbol, but it is also functional.

Although the area of the glass surface is enormous, the energy efficiency of the home is optimum, thanks to the solar panels on the roof and the way the structure is sited. The skeleton of the building is metal. The façade is green-covered metal panels.

Two details of the façade.

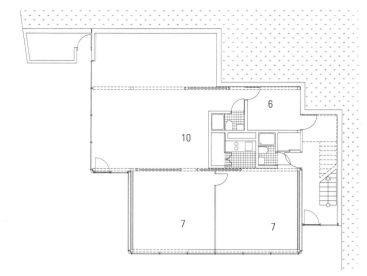

First floor

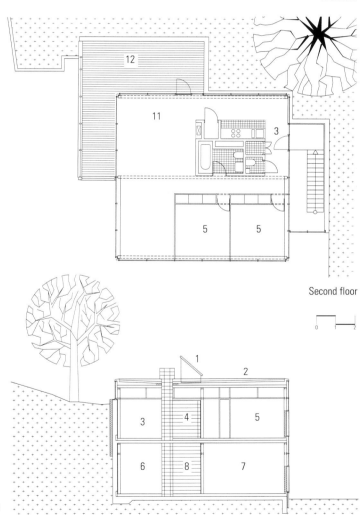

Second floor

1. Solar energy panels
2. Ceiling
3. Kitchen
4. Bathroom
5. Bedrooms
6. Storage room
7. Guest bedroom
8. Bathroom
9. Entrance
10. Workshop
11. Empty space-warehouse
12. Roof

Section

Pictures of the house
under construction.

Sketch showing the different
conceptual phases of the
project. The slope of the ground
was employed to design a
house based on ecological
principles.

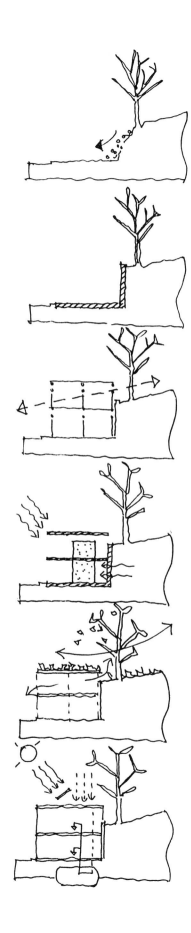

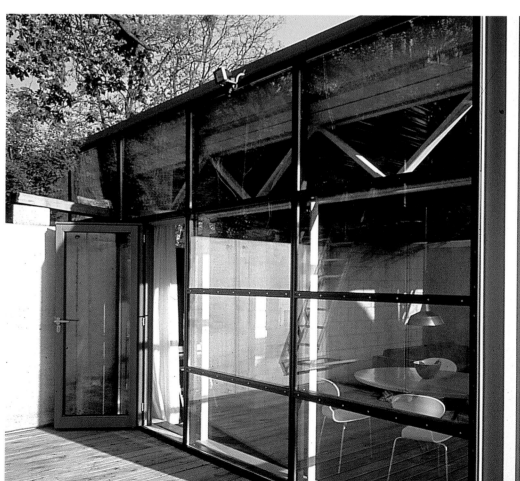

On the left, pictures of the architect's studio and its open-plan design. The panels dividing the workshop into different areas do not reach the ceiling. On this page, views of the home, where the rooms are more walled in to give the simple structure a sense of intimacy and privacy. The entire project was quick and inexpensive.

Page 130: different views of the building showing the metal skeleton. Prefabricated pieces were fitted on a framework.

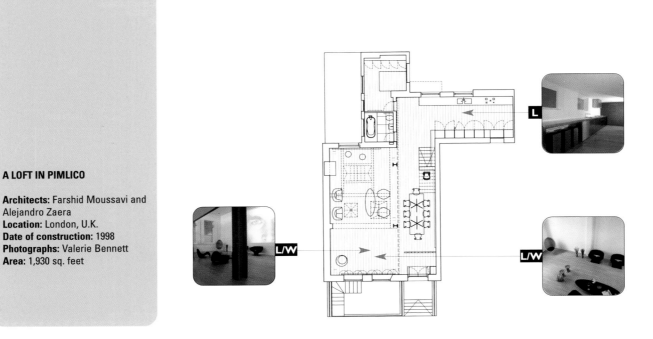

A LOFT IN PIMLICO

Architects: Farshid Moussavi and Alejandro Zaera
Location: London, U.K.
Date of construction: 1998
Photographs: Valerie Bennett
Area: 1,930 sq. feet

MULTI-FUNCTIONAL DWELLING Farshid Moussavi and Alejandro Zaera

lthough architects Farshid Moussavi and Alejandro Zaera only work at home part time, this multifunctional space has been included here because it allows few clear distinctions between public and private activities and between rooms for night or day time use. The L-shaped loft in the London neighborhood of Pimlico has ceilings which are nearly 16 feet high, with a somewhat lower-ceilinged wing leading directly to the street. The main space, which includes the living and dining areas, connects to the outside through two very tall windows and to an interior patio through another large window. The two-story main wall has been put to good use, giving the room the feel of an art gallery.

Given this favored setting, the architects exploited the features of the loft to the hilt. Some 645 square feet of floor space was gained by creating a mezzanine floor to house a bedroom which can be divided by means of sliding panels, a bathroom, and book shelves visible from the main space.

A limited palette of materials was used to give the project a feeling of unity and to avoid detracting from the inherent quality of the space. All the walls and ceilings were painted white, except the end wall of the kitchen, which was finished in slate. Wide, solid oak tiles were found to be perfect for the floor. The bathroom flooring, the toilet and bath are sandstone. All the steel was painted gray; the hinged doors were varnished in matte black and the sliding doors in white, like the walls.

Cupboards cover the walls, opening from floor to ceiling and playing with the geometric precision of the space. The furniture, on the other hand, was selected for its complex curves, which contrast with the planes typical of the dwelling. Designs by the architects themselves are combined with works by the masters in the field.

Lighting, always indirect and reflected back off the walls, is provided by incandescent white tubes and halogen spotlights. A central panel controls different light sequences through a programmable computer.

View of the library that is used by both architects as a studio and workshop.

The bookcase, with its shelves painted white, extends from the lower floor to the loft. The TV and video equipment that the owners use for their work is placed on top.

Detail of one of the corners of the living room on the lower floor.

The main two-story wall is used by the architects as a screen where they can project images of their own work.

1. Entrance hall
2. Living room
3. Dining room
4. Kitchen
5. Bedrooms
6. Bathroom
7. Studio
8. Terrace

Page 138: Top: view of one of the slides that the architects use as an inspirational source.
Bottom: detail of the kitchen.

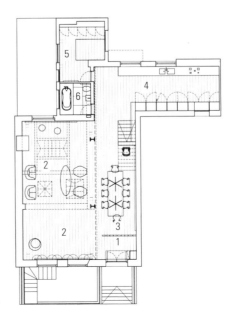

Lower floor

Mezzanine floor

Section

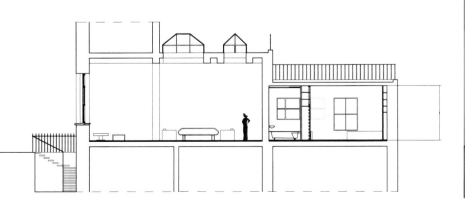

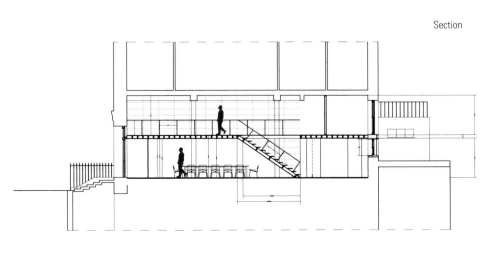

Section

The bedrooms are bathed in the natural light that flows in through the generous windows, which offer views of Pimlico.

Previous page: Top: the staircae leading to one of the working areas. Bottom: View of the kitchen on the lower floor.

The stone bath was
designed by the
architects, with the
intention of
maintaining constraint
throughout the house.

THE MUZI FALCONE HOUSE

Architect: Antonio Zanuso
Collaborator: Anna Muzi Falcone
Location: Milan, Italy
Date of construction: 1998
Photographs: Henry Bourne/
Speranza
Area: 2,700 sq. feet

A PAINTER'S LOFT Antonio Zanuso

The home of artist Anna Muzi Falcone occupies the third floor of a turn-of-the-century industrial building in a picturesque area of Milan. The architect for the renovation, Antonio Zanuso, and his young client are close friends, so it not surprising that the styles and whims of both are expressed in the final result.

The loft is divided into two areas which form an L. One of these areas adjoins the building's interior patio. The other enjoys views of the city. Zanuso organized the space logically, using a layout free of physical and visual obstacles.

The entire loft is bright, thanks to the large windows. The entrance area leads into an enormous kitchen, which retains the building's original industrial ambience, then into a long passage to the living room and two studios. Two bedrooms and a bathroom are located on the right.

The work area has no doors, and the relationship between the studios and the rest of the space is emphasized by a gray resin floor.

The very high ceiling allowed the architect to create an intermediate floor where the most private rooms are located. This level is accessible by two staircases, one from the studio and the other from the passage.

The main bedroom on this floor overlooks the living room through interior windows. Next to the bedroom is a bath and a private dressing room.

The project was conceived as a space for living, working, and holding social gatherings: a neutral space in which the client's paintings would catch one's eye among the furnishings. The owner planned the decor herself, mixing original pieces with items picked up in street markets and antique shops.

The working area. It is a long narrow space with movable furniture that allows multiple distribution options.

Above and below: views of the living room. The furnishings and decoration combine original pieces designed by recognized artists and objects found in street markets. The owner, painter Anna Muzi Falcone, designed the interior decoration.

Above: the dinning room. The concept behind the project was the creation of a flexible space in which to live, work, and hold social get-togethers.

Bottom left: view of the corridor connecting working and living spaces. Bottom right: colorful detail of the materials used by the painter.

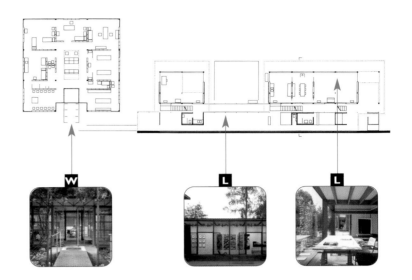

A RESIDENCE NEAR PADERBORN

Architects: Herzog & Partner
Collaborators: Reinhold Tobey,
Anneliese and Peter Latz,
Andrea Heigl
Location: Paderborn, Germany
Date of construction: 1998
Photographs: Dieter Leistner/Artur
Area: 2,420 sq. feet

A DOCTOR'S HOME AND OFFICE   Herzog & Partner

The first part of this project on the banks of the Lippe River near the town of Paderborn in Germany, was constructed in the 1980s. The building, a one-story high square housing the office of a doctor specializing in internal medicine, is divided into nine sections of 270 square feet each. The main consulting room is lit by a skylight which also provides light for the entryway and corridors.

Panels open and close to control ventilation and regulate the amount of sunlight that enters.

The glazed corners reinforce the building's relationship with the magnificent landscape in the area and accentuate the floor's diagonals. The interior strongly reflects the metal framework, which distributes weight through a wooden beam system.

In the mid-nineties, a residence was erected along the approach to the office. The façade, which overlooks the access route, is a continuous wall of reinforced concrete that provides visual and thermal isolation. The house's layout is simple: rooms following one after another, varying in function, materials, light, and temperature.

Inside, along the wall, a passageway connects the different rooms and doubles as an art gallery. During the coldest months, when the large windows are closed, it becomes a greenhouse, with a heating system under the floor.

From outside, the home appears to be of uniform elevation, but on the south side, steps provide a change in both level and character. The high-ceilinged display area is restrained and cold, while the living areas, finished in wood and painted in reddish tones, are warm and comfortable.

The bathroom, sauna, and toilets are in rooms of unfinished concrete along the central axis.

Spatial continuity is enhanced by glass in the ceilings and side walls. Although the project is dominated by simple geometry, the outcome is rich in sensations which are enhanced by the close relationship between indoors and outdoors.

Access to the living area.

Working area | Living area

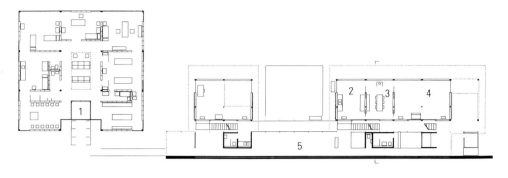

First floor

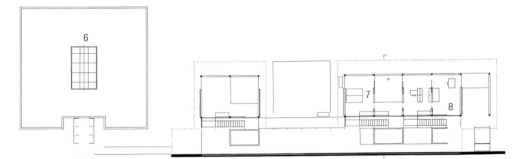

Second floor

1. Office
2. Kitchen
3. Dining room
4. Living room
5. Corridor
6. Skylight
7. Bedroom
8. Personal office

Next page: three views of the interior of the building where the doctor works. All this working area has direct access to the garden.

The building on the left is the living area. The one on the right is the working space.

The exterior façade combines glass windows and wood panels that can both be opened to regulate the entrance of sunlight and fresh air.

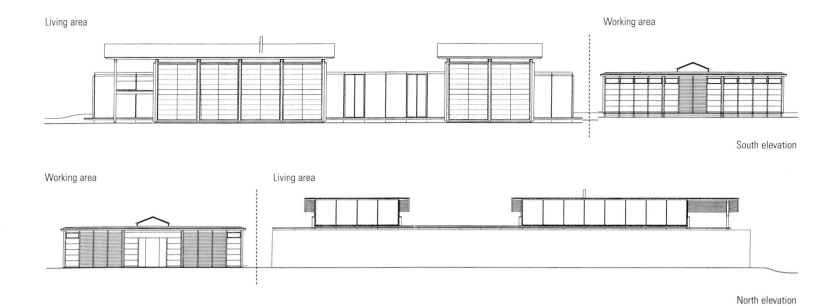

Living area

Working area

South elevation

Working area

Living area

North elevation

Views of the living room.

The large front window provides a close relationship with the outside. Only a few pillars spoil the illusion that the interior and the garden are part of one continuous space.

THE ALONSO PLANAS HOUSE

Architects: Carlos Ferrater and Joan Guibernau
Location: Esplugues de Llobregat, Spain
Date of construction: 1998
Photographs: Eugeni Pons
Area: 5,860 sq. feet

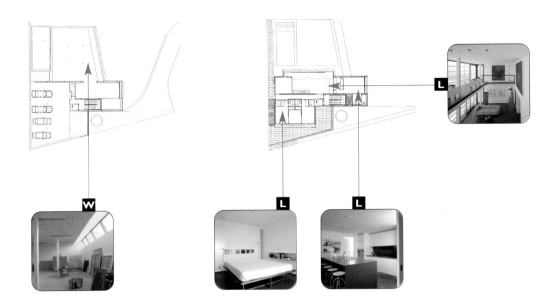

A HOUSE AND WORKSHOP FOR A PAINTER AND A SCULPTOR   C. Ferrater and J. Guibernau

The Alonso Planas house lies on a steep, elongated plot of land near a mountain ridge. The city of Barcelona is spread out below while, to the southwest, the flat lands on either side of the Llobregat River fade into the distance. The views are magnificent in every direction.

The main part of the residence was situated on the upper part of the slope, with level areas on both sides of the building, resulting in clear views of the valley. The long, narrow structure has three stories to make family life easier. On each level, the interior blends with the exterior. The lower has direct access to the swimming pool and sun deck. The middle floor leads out to the garden, while the upper floor adjoins the more secluded and intimate terraces hidden behind the walls.

The basement, dug into the mountain, contains the entrance, garage, and utility rooms. Space created by the building's extended shape has been used to good advantage, with painting and sculpture studios. Light streams in steadily through a large horizontal opening defined by a concrete-and-glass piece, allowing a view of the upper patio. No partitions interrupt the space, which remains open and flexible.

The walls, flagstones, and canopies are concrete. Specially ordered white bricks are used around the windows, with long pieces used as lintels and latticework admitting fresh breezes and more light. The woodwork is teak; openings employ a complicated system of mechanically adjustable hanging slats.

The effect sought was one of serenity. That the detailed design could almost go unnoticed attests to the architect's achievement of this objective.

Parking entrance.

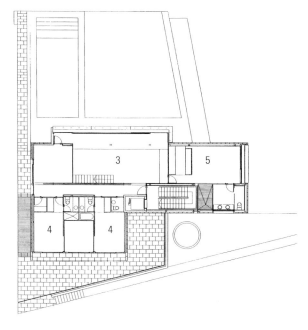

Lower floor:
1. Garage
2. Atelier

Middle floor:
3. Living room
4. Bedrooms
5. Kitchen-living room

Two views of the exterior: the main
entrance and detail of the east façade.

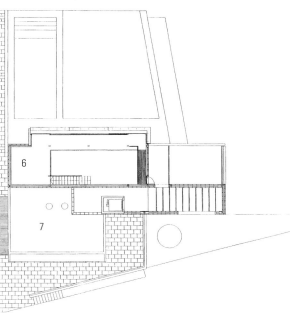

Upper floor:
6. Library
7. Terrace

The workshop, partially below ground, is illuminated by large, high windows. This long strip of glazing provides constant ethereal light, ideal for painting. This is the space where the painter and sculptor spents most of her working time.

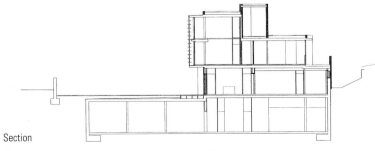

Section

View of the living room from the second floor.

A high-ceilinged area accommodates a living room and dining room on the ground floor and the library on the upper floor. Moreover, the entire corridor bordering the glass façade is used to exhibit unique objects.

One of the building's walls has been used for the kitchen. The sink is part of a wide unit which includes a counter and table for preparing quick meals.

The bedroom is a neutral space where the furnishings play a prominent role. The decorative objects, such as the paintings and lamps, are especially suggestive.

The woodwork of the living room doors and windows is teak. The glass is shielded by a complex system of mechanically controlled sliding, suspended slats. Other areas are covered by latticework which allows ventilation and light.

A MOBILE STUDIO IN REIMSCHEID

Architects: Kalhöfer & Korschildgen
Collaborator: Andreas Hack
Location: Reimscheid, Germany
Date of construction: 1997
Photographs: Wilfried Dechau
Area: 430 sq. feet

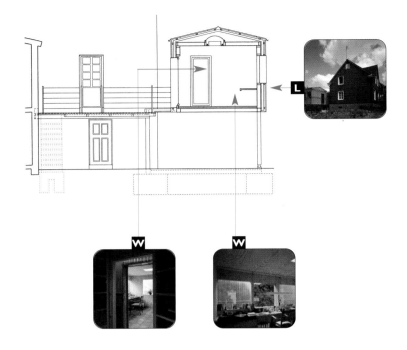

A GARDEN STUDIO   Kalhöfer & Korschildgen

The clients, two journalists, had rented out the upper floor of their residence and wanted to increase the living space, just three rooms, remaining to them. They needed a flexible working environment which could assume a different function when the guest moved out. The young architects who worked on the project came up with a radical and striking solution: a studio on tracks which could be placed in different locations at whim.

Bearing in mind the homeowners' fondness for their garden, the architectural team decided that the studio would be in direct contact with the open space, placing it in a vacant corner beside the house and allowing it to extend over the lot. So, during the summer, the structure is separated from the house on sliding tracks, and in the winter it adjoins the residence. In both cases it exploits the advantages of its location. From June through September it creates an open air terrace while, in winter, the homeowners can go to work without overcoats.

The house can be reconverted season by season and, the day the guest leaves, the changes can easily be undone and the studio can be converted into a greenhouse. The furniture was designed so that eliminating the work space would not involve exorbitant expenditures.

The studio is modeled on an expansion carried out in the fifties.

The external skin is made of transparent, wavy PVC sheets which keep out the bitter cold. The interior skin is made of thermal insulation and plywood.

A coat of silvery paint reflects heat and rounds off the structure's kinetic aspect. The electrical and communication systems are located in the space between the PVC panels, the building's exposed neural network.

The studio and working area is a movable piece that can be separated from the main living building when necessary.

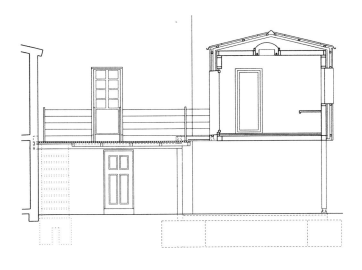

Elevations

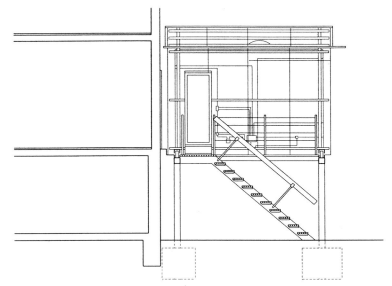

Construction section

The layout shows the rail
system that allows the studio
to be arranged most suitably. In
summer, the terrace is cleared
to create a space where the
landscape can be enjoyed.

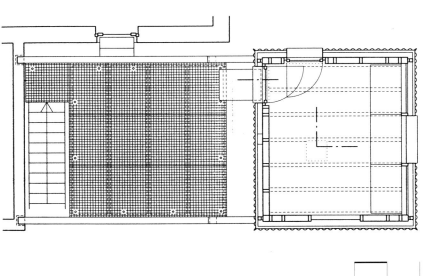

First floor

0   1   2

The mobile studio. In summer, entry is through a side door. In winter, it is through the house door so you do not have to go outside to get to work.

The inside of the studio is covered in wood. Large windows and a skylight allow abundant light to enter. The wavy PVC sheets soften the sun's rays, providing a warm, serene atmosphere.

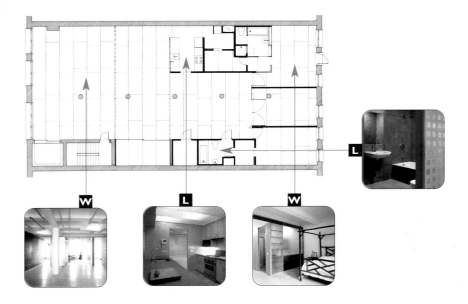

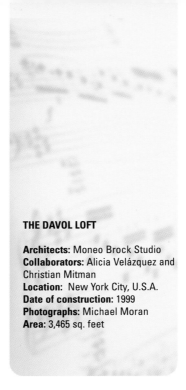

THE DAVOL LOFT

Architects: Moneo Brock Studio
Collaborators: Alicia Velázquez and
Christian Mitman
Location: New York City, U.S.A.
Date of construction: 1999
Photographs: Michael Moran
Area: 3,465 sq. feet

A STUDIO/RESIDENCE FOR TWO PROFESSIONALS   Moneo Brock Studio

The building which contains the Davol Loft is one of many being renovated in the old industrial areas of lower Manhattan. The factories of bygone years are being converted into dwellings, new apartment buildings are going up, and humanizing features such as parks, walkways, and bicycle paths are being laid out along the Hudson river.

This project began with an empty rectangular space having the typical characteristics of a loft (columns down the center supporting beams that stretch across the building, enormous windows, ceilings more than ten feet high). This spatial configuration presented a challenge with respect to integrating living space and a fully operational work area, especially since it was essential that natural light reach the center of the apartment.

The clients, a pair of professional musicians, needed separate bedrooms with attached baths, a kitchen, a small storage room, and a large open space for the living room, plus a flexible work area for each. The architects, knowing the clients' minds, worked artfully, on a modest budget, allowing for the possibility that better-quality finishes could be introduced in the future.

The architects placed the service areas against the windowless north and south walls. They avoided total visual separation of these rooms from the rest of the loft by treating them like modules inserted into a container. Partitions do not reach all the way to the ceiling and iridescent materials are used, creating magnificent reflective patterns that accentuate the lightness of the components.

There is flexibility in how the apartment can be used, emphasizing either the personal or the professional. Mobile, translucent panels substitute for fixed dividers. A new material, Panelite, was critical to the loft design. It is not only translucent, but its coloration varies with the light falling on it. Rails make the system even more adaptable. The panels can easily be moved to enclose different areas and can double up to achieve greater opacity.

The clients' attitude was crucial to the success of the project. From the beginning they accepted the risk and challenge of experimenting with new materials. Their enthusiasm made it possible to create this opalescent oasis from which they can admire the sunset.

Typical structure of a loft: columns
supporting beams, big windows...

Section

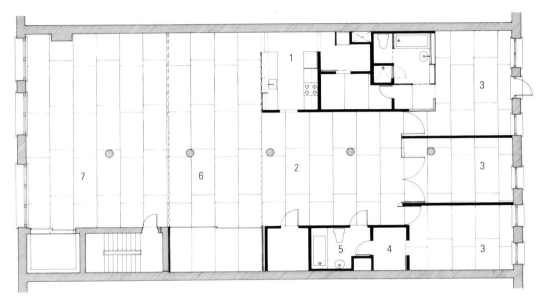

Floor layout

1. Kitchen
2. Dinning room
3. Bedrooms
4. Dressing room
5. Bathroom
6. Living room
7. Rehearsing room

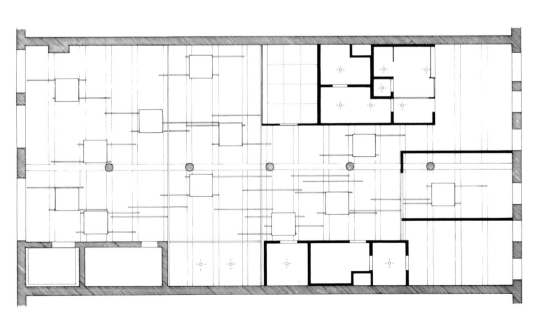

Floor with projecting roof

The invention by the architects of a translucent material called Panelite was key for the design of all partitions.

0   1   2

Some of the partitions are moveable, making it easy to redistribute the apartment's space.

The panels' translucency permits a distinctive spatial relationship and avoids permanent compartmentalization.

Bathroom.

The finishes produce a
pattern of colors, reflections,
and transparencies.
The extraordinary impression
left by the space is the fruit
of intense experimentation
with the materials.

Entrance hall. At the back, part of the multiuse - working space.

The kitchen and dinning room are integrated in the living room.

This large, multiuse space must meet certain acoustic requirements because the clients often use it to rehearse.

Bottom right: the bathroom was built with stone surfaces and translucent panels. It acts like a lamp for the bedroom where it is located.

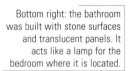

The translucent interior partitions allow partial observation of activities in the various rooms. From the bedroom, the kitchen shelves can be seen.